The Labor Market Experience of Workers with Disabilities

The ADA and Beyond

The Labor Market Experience of Workers with Disabilities

The ADA and Beyond

Julie L. Hotchkiss

2003

W.E. Upjohn Institute for Employment Research
Kalamazoo, Michigan

Library of Congress Cataloging-in-Publication Data

Hotchkiss, Julie L.
    The labor market experience of workers with disabilities / Julie L.
Hotchkiss.
        p. cm.
    ISBN 0-88099-251-4 (pbk. : alk. paper)—ISBN 0-88099-252-2
(hardcover : alk. paper)
        1. Handicapped—Employment—United States. 2.
Handicapped—Employment—Government policy—United States. 3. Labor
market—United States. 4. Discrimination in employment—Law and
legislation—United States. 5. Handicapped—Legal status, laws,
etc.—United States. 6. United States. Americans with Disabilities Act
of 1990. I. Title.
    HD7256.U5 H68 2002
    331.5′9′0973—dc21   2002151811

The facts presented in this study and the observations and viewpoints expressed are
the sole responsibility of the authors. They do not necessarily represent positions of
the W.E. Upjohn Institute for Employment Research.

Cover design by J.R. Underhill.
Index prepared by Nancy Humphreys.
Printed in the United States of America.

Contents

Figures

Tables

Acknowledgments

This research would not have been possible without the financial support of the W.E. Upjohn Institute for Employment Research. I also appreciate the assistance and comments of the Upjohn Institute staff economists. Allan Hunt, Kevin Hollenbeck, and Stephen Woodbury were particularly helpful. In addition, I would like to thank the following people who were instrumental in the completion of this project: Jack McNeil and Vic Valdisera of the U.S. Census Bureau, Bob McIntire of the U.S. Bureau of Labor Statistics, David Autor, Christopher Bollinger, Barry Hirsch, Doug Kruse, David Macpherson, Robert Margo, Walter Oi, and my colleagues Robert E. Moore and M. Melinda Pitts. The research assistance and contributions of Ludmila Rovba are without measure. Generosa Kagaruki also provided valuable research help. Lastly, I would like to dedicate this book to my parents, Burt and Nonnie Hotchkiss.

Preface

As of July 26, 1994, employers with 15 or more employees have been subject to the labor market provisions of the Americans with Disabilities Act (ADA). Employers with 25 or more employees became subject to the provisions in 1992. For people with disabilities, the ADA gives civil rights protections similar to those provided to individuals on the basis of race, color, sex, national origin, age, and religion. It guarantees equal opportunity in public accommodations, employment, transportation, state and local government services, and telecommunications. This book focuses exclusively on the labor market provisions of the ADA. Its goal is to provide a comprehensive analysis of the current labor market experience of American workers with disabilities and an assessment of the impact the ADA has had on that experience.

The ADA prohibits discrimination in all employment practices, including job application procedures, hiring, firing, advancement, compensation, training, and other terms, conditions, and privileges of employment. It applies to recruitment, advertising, tenure, layoff, leave, fringe benefits, and all other employment-related activities. It is hoped that, by breaking down the labor market barriers that Americans with disabilities have faced in the past, we will all benefit from an untapped source of productivity, the resulting increase in purchasing power, and a simultaneous savings on disability payments.

Most previous studies have either focused on only one dimension of the labor market experience (e.g., wages or employment levels), evaluated that experience at only one point in time, or focused on the labor supply impact of disability policies. However, one's labor market experience has many dimensions; this research explores the labor market experience across those dimensions and across time. The result is a more complete picture of what Americans with disabilities can expect as participants in the labor market and of whether this experience has been affected by the passage of the ADA. Given that policies such as the ADA are designed to affect the lives of groups of individuals, the experience of disabled workers as a whole is evaluated rather than the experience of any one person.

Much of the earlier research on workers with disabilities relates to issues of labor supply, such as policies that shape workforce participation decisions of the disabled, circumstances that improve the chances of injured workers returning to work, or details of the special needs of the disabled (e.g., access to health care, personal assistance) that might hinder their entrance into the workforce. While the analyses contained in this book do not ignore labor supply issues, the focus is on more direct evidence of the existence of and changes in *barriers* to a positive labor market experience. Barriers are defined here as parts of the labor market experience controlled by the employer, which are the aspects directly addressed by the ADA and can be considered demand-side factors.

When a policy such as the ADA finally comes to fruition, there is often a question as to whether any observed changes in the experience of those affected by the law can be attributed to the law itself or whether changes in experience merely reflect the environment in which the law was passed. If the latter were true, this would not be to say that the ADA was unnecessary, just that it did not have the dramatic impact some opponents probably feared because the changes were already occurring. It is also possible that no change in experience of the disabled will be seen leading up to the passage or following implementation of the ADA. If this is the case and if the experience of disabled workers in the labor market remains inferior to that of the nondisabled, then we clearly have to look beyond the ADA to improve that labor market situation.

The analyses in this book show that while disabled workers are making progress in some dimensions of their labor market experience, the ADA does not seem to have had a striking impact in either a positive or negative direction. Expanding or strengthening incentives to enter the labor force, providing training focused in high-growth and high-earnings occupations, and assistance in screening and matching workers with appropriate jobs are policies that would capitalize on the recent progress made by disabled workers and move them in the direction of greater labor market gains.

1
Introduction

DISABILITY LEGISLATION IN THE UNITED STATES

The excitement, fear, and general controversy surrounding the passage of the Americans with Disabilities Act (ADA) in 1990 might lead some to believe that this was the first time the United States had ever confronted the issue of potential discrimination against or differential treatment of people with disabilities. To the contrary, the nation has demonstrated some concern through legislation for individuals with disabilities since the 1920s. Not until the ADA, however, was there as sweeping a mandate, theoretically touching multiple dimensions of a disabled person's life.

The National Civilian Vocational Rehabilitation Act became law in 1920, was amended several times, then became the Vocational Rehabilitation Act in 1954. Public Law 93-112 transformed it into the Rehabilitation Act of 1973 (sections 503–504), which prohibits discrimination against the disabled by any program receiving federal assistance and requires federal agencies to take affirmative action to employ handicapped individuals. In addition, the act dictates that companies having contracts of a certain size with the federal government ($10,000 or more, as of 1998) publicly state that the organization takes affirmative action to employ and accommodate workers with disabilities. Executive Order 12086 in 1978 reassigned enforcement of the act to the U.S. Department of Labor. This strengthened the position of disabled and veteran workers by placing the regulation enforcement in line with protection from discrimination based on race, color, religion, sex, or national origin.[1] So, while nondiscrimination against and employment of disabled workers have been of concern for firms doing business with the federal government for some time, it was not until the passage of the ADA that all firms in the United States (employing 15 or more people) would be held to the same standard regarding employment and accommodation of individuals with disabilities.

In many ways individual states have taken the lead in providing workplace opportunities for the disabled. By 1990, all states had passed antidiscrimination legislation covering employment by state agencies and often employment by any firm doing business with the state.[2] In addition, nearly all states by that time covered private employers in some form or another, and many states covered all employment, including that by very small firms (fewer than 15 workers). Common exclusions from the discrimination legislation included religious organizations, social clubs, family members, American Indian tribes, and farm or domestic workers. Details of when each state passed legislation related to treatment of the disabled in the workplace and the exclusions of those laws are in Appendix D.

The Rehabilitation Act of 1973, and the concern already expressed at the state level about the employment opportunities of disabled workers, culminated in the passage of the ADA in 1990. This act was unlike others before it, in that it provided for the civil rights of people with disabilities in the same way that all citizens are protected against discrimination based on race, color, sex, national origin, age, and religion. The ADA requires that employers treat workers, and potential workers, with disabilities identically to those without disabilities, with regard to hiring, compensation, and other aspects of employment. In addition, employers must make reasonable efforts to accommodate the nature of the worker's disability in connection with the performance of the worker's job. Owners of places of public accommodation are required to provide facilities (e.g., entrances, elevators, bathrooms) fit for the disabled, and to provide services in such a way that people with disabilities are not restricted from receiving those services (e.g., requiring a driver's license as the only way to provide proof of identification discriminates against the vision impaired). Public accommodation also includes equal access through telecommunication, such as access to the Internet. While admittedly only a small part of the entire legislation, the implications and impact of the labor market provisions (Title I) of the ADA provide the focus of this book.

Any interpretation of the effect of the ADA or recommendations for enhancements must take into account policies already in place that may or may not influence a disabled worker's labor market experience. The Social Security Administration manages two cash payment programs for Americans with disabilities. Such programs are of great concern regarding labor market analyses for two main reasons. First, cash payment programs might crowd out labor market activity, and

second, they may be structured in such a way that labor market participation is discouraged. The Social Security Disability Insurance Program (SSDI) provides benefits to workers who have been able to make
enough contributions through the social security Federal Insurance
Contributions Act (FICA) tax paid on their previous earnings. The
Supplemental Security Income Program (SSI) is available to disabled
Americans who have limited income and resources. The eligibility
rules for payments from these two programs differ, but they both require the applicant to be either not working or earning less than some
specified amount. Both programs include incentives to get recipients
back into the labor force. These incentives include a trial work period
where some or all of the payments are retained for a certain period of
time; continuation of Medicaid or Medicare even if cash payments have
ended because of high earnings; reimbursement of impairment-related
work expenses; exclusion of certain income from the earnings test if
set aside for future self-sufficiency, such as education or starting a
business; and referral and payment for vocational rehabilitation. Many
of these incentives were only adopted recently as part of the Ticket to
Work and Work Incentives Improvement Act of 1999 (Public Law 106-
170).

The goals of the Ticket to Work initiative complement the goals of
the ADA. Whereas these work incentive programs are designed to
encourage the disabled to seek jobs and become self-sufficient, the
ADA is intended to provide an environment in which these efforts are
met with support and reasonable assistance.

POLICY ISSUES

The United States has a history of enacting legislation with strong
social content, expressing society's ethics and morals. Child labor
laws and other civil rights legislation fall into this category. One could
argue that such laws are grounded in economic concerns. For example,
discrimination against workers with disabilities or against African
Americans robs our economy of the efficient allocation and use of
valuable resources. Also, with the prohibition of child labor, children
really have no other option but to attend school, raising the human
capital of our economy overall. While these arguments have merit in

fact, it is also true that as a society we support these laws from an emotional and moral level. For example, the 1991 Harris poll on Public Attitudes toward People with Disabilities demonstrated that while most people were not even aware that the ADA had been passed (62 percent), they felt overwhelmingly (95 percent) that "Given how many difficulties disabled people face in their daily lives, the least society can do is make an extra effort to improve things for them."[3]   In addition, 81 percent of those surveyed thought that there should be an affirmative action program for people with disabilities. These are responses not entirely driven by economic concerns.

When legislation is propelled by an evolution of ethical and moral concerns, we must face the question of whether it serves as a statement of where we (as a society) are rather than as a prediction of where we are going.[4] For example, the establishment of a minimum age for employment (child labor laws) has been shown to have had little impact on the decline of child labor in the early part of the 20th century (Moehling 1999). The implication is that legislation of strong social content, rather than precipitating social change, is often actually a *response to* social change. In other words, the ADA might merely serve as a reflection of our moral and ethical beliefs rather than as a tool with which to improve the condition of a segment of society. Some argue that the ADA is "feel-good legislation that promises more than it delivers" (Jay 1990, p. 23). A major criticism is that the ADA is absent of specifics necessary for effective compliance, particularly on the subject of what constitutes "undue hardship," which serves as the measure of whether a firm must make the physical environment, service, or employment "accessible." Some interpret the refusal of Congress to tackle the difficult issues that were sure to arise as indication that the ADA's primary function was merely to be a statement of our morals. In addition, an amendment to the ADA that would have disallowed jury trials and punitive damages for disabled victims of discrimination (an amendment that would have been a clear sign that the ADA was not meant to have any teeth), was only narrowly defeated (Jay 1990).

The implication, if the ADA serves merely as a statement of where we are, is that no impact of the law will be detected because, for the most part, we have already adopted the principles and practices laid out by the legislation. This outcome, then, begs the question of whether the ADA or child labor laws are necessary, or whether such legislation is simply an expensive declaration of our morals. Even though one could argue that these laws might merely be statements of something we already knew, an even stronger argument might be made that public acknowledgment of a collective moral foundation serves an important purpose, one beyond quantification in economic terms.[5] These laws strongly proclaim our social values and provide a legal mechanism with which to arrest the activities of those who have not yet adopted those ethics.

In order to address whether the ADA merely serves as a statement of where we are rather than as a prediction of where we are headed, the analyses in this book will focus on two basic questions. First, how are disabled workers faring (relative to nondisabled workers) at any given point in time, and is their relative experience in the labor market improving? Second, did the ADA have any discernible impact on the relative experience of disabled workers? These questions will be asked in relation to as many dimensions of the labor market experience as possible.

The questioning does not stop with the analyses, however. If it is discovered that the ADA has had or is having a positive impact on the labor market experience of disabled workers, then the ADA is accomplishing what it was designed to do. If the ADA has not had a measurable effect on the relative labor market experience of disabled workers, and if their experience still falls short of that of nondisabled workers, then we may need to look toward additional or different legislation, specifically targeted at improving those dimensions identified as the most lacking.

FOCUS AND STRATEGY OF ANALYSES

This book is concerned with the labor market implications and impact of the ADA. In addition to the multiple dimensions of the potential effect of the ADA on disabled workers, there are at least as many more ways in which the ADA influences the lives of *all* disabled Americans; these other outcomes are not the subject of the present discussion, but may in fact amount to a much greater overall impact than that felt by the disabled in the labor market. The strategy of analysis followed here for documenting the impact of the ADA on the labor market experience of disabled workers has been to assemble as much information on as many dimensions of that experience as possible. The major contribution of the analyses that follow is the wide-ranging coverage and synthesis of a massive amount of information in such a way as to make recommendations for policy. The emphasis has not been on developing *new* ways to examine the labor market experience of the disabled, but to *broaden* that examination.

The focus is on labor demand issues, defining the environment that the disabled might face. As a result, the analyses of employment and wages, for example, will correspond to what a disabled person might encounter upon entering the labor market. The conclusions will not be conditional on the labor supply decisions of the disabled, but will take those decisions into account in presenting unconditional results that apply to the population of the disabled, instead of merely to the sample (of workers) on which the estimates are obtained. Other analyses, such as the incidence of voluntary part-time employment, job separation, or job search experience, will be generalizable only to that population for which the issues are relevant: the part-time employed, the employed only, or the unemployed only. These sample limitations are legitimate and logical given the population for which such questions are relevant.

It is important to remember that the purpose of the labor market provisions of the ADA was to break down barriers to the disabled and to improve their experiences in the labor market. Although perhaps expected, the alteration of various voluntary behaviors (such as labor force participation) was not the goal of these provisions. A fair analysis of the ADA should only involve an evaluation of what it was designed to do. Regardless of its intent, however, any policy can have unintended consequences that should also be addressed.

Outline of the Book

Chapter 2 explores employment outcomes among the disabled. Both joint labor force and employment and unconditional employment probabilities are examined for the entire sample of disabled individuals, controlling for selection into the labor force. The availability of firm size and the phased-in nature of the ADA are exploited in a differences-in-differences analysis. Results by type of disability are also presented. The joint labor force participation and employment probability for disabled persons declined relative to this joint outcome among nondisabled individuals after the ADA was implemented. However, the unconditional (i.e., controlling for selection into the labor market) employment probability did not change post-ADA, relative to the experience of the nondisabled. The source of the deteriorating joint outcome is explored in some depth. In addition, employment among the disabled was found to shift more toward larger firms than did employment among nondisabled workers, suggesting that implementation of the ADA and the financial ability (of larger firms) to accommodate workers' disabilities mattered in the employment experience of disabled workers.

Chapter 3 looks at the wages earned by disabled and nondisabled workers. A pooled, cross-sectional analysis suggests that wages among disabled workers fell post-ADA, relative to wages among the nondisabled. In addition, a standard decomposition of the wage differential observed between disabled and nondisabled workers is performed. The availability of benefits is also explored through a simple probit analysis. While the overall compensation experience of disabled workers is found to be deteriorating relative to nondisabled workers (in both wages and availability of employer-sponsored fringe benefits), the degree to which discrimination might be used to explain this differential is also declining. It is found, however, that wages of disabled workers explicitly covered by the ADA (based on the size of their employers) have not changed post-ADA, relative to their noncovered counterparts, suggesting the overall lower wages among the disabled are being driven by more than accommodation costs.

A number of job quality issues are addressed in Chapter 4. First, hours of work and the incidence of part-time employment and type of part-time employment among disabled and nondisabled workers are explored. Second, the distribution of workers across occupations and industries is compared using a popular distributional index. Third, the representation of disabled workers in high-growth and high-wage jobs is evaluated. This chapter presents evidence that while the incidence of part-time employment is increasing for disabled workers, relative to nondisabled workers, the incidence of *voluntary* part-time employment is driving that increase, particularly among workers with mental disorders. The degree of dissimilarity and the growth in dissimilarity in occupation and industry distributions of disabled and nondisabled workers over the 1981–2000 period are striking. While showing some improvement since 1992, this is of concern since disabled workers also appear to be concentrated in low-growth, low-wage occupations.

Job separation and unemployment experiences of the disabled are explored in Chapter 5. Results from a multinomial logit find that, among individuals who have separated from their job, disabled workers are more likely to have separated voluntarily and less likely to have separated involuntarily than nondisabled workers. A similar analysis then finds that, among the unemployed, disabled workers are more likely to be reentrants and new entrants into the labor market than nondisabled workers. A duration analysis shows that disabled job seekers are searching on average three weeks longer before finding a job than similar nondisabled persons, and that most of the difference in observed search length is explained by differences in individual characteristics. Taken together, these results suggest that while the endowments or characteristics of disabled and nondisabled workers appear to be valued equally, employers may be going to greater lengths to discern the fit of a disabled worker's skill set with a particular job, thus leading to longer searches, a better match, and less chance that a separation is for involuntary reasons.

Chapter 6 explores the impact of state-level legislation on wages, employment, and hours of disabled workers in different states. The analyses in this chapter exploit the differential timing of protective legislation across a number of states. The results are consistent and support the findings from Chapters 2, 3, and 4 on these same issues. Namely, wages decline and overall employment probabilities are unchanged among disabled workers, post-legislation, relative to nondisabled workers. In addition, part-time employment among disabled workers increases post-legislation. These results suggest that the wage and part-time employment effect of the ADA may have been much greater if the state legislation had not already absorbed some if its potential impact.

Chapter 7 synthesizes the results of the previous chapters around policy implications and recommendations. It is suggested that three directions be followed to further enhance the labor market experience of disabled workers: 1) provide incentives to the disabled to enter the labor force and relief to employers for the cost of accommodating these individuals; 2) expand the support of resources available for disabled workers to increase their general human capital and ability to move into high-paying occupations; and 3) provide mechanisms by which employers and disabled workers can find each other and determine the appropriateness of the employment match.

Data Details and Estimation Issues

The combined Current Population Survey (CPS) Annual Earnings files for the months of March, April, May, and June, for the years 1981 through 2000, were used to obtain demographic data, employment status, earnings, details related to the respondent's job, and location information to control for local labor market conditions. These CPS Annual Earnings files were matched with the March CPS survey for each year to obtain data on disability status, other sources of income, and labor market information available for the previous year. This strategy resulted in a sample four times larger than any single month of current labor market statistics, yielding greater confidence in the precision of the results.

Some have questioned whether self-reported disability status (as in the CPS) suffers from endogeneity (e.g., Parsons 1980; Haveman and Wolfe 1984). For example, it may be the case that someone less likely to enter the labor market or to be employed is also more likely to report the presence of a disability (i.e., the disability indicator and error term of the regression are not independent). Stern (1989) finds that "any bias due to potential endogeneity is small" (p. 363). Of course, endogeneity may be more of a concern since the passage of the ADA. As will be addressed in Chapter 2, endogeneity among the population as a whole may be a greater problem than among only labor force participants (also see Kreider 1999). Additional criticism has been lobbed at the use of the traditional "work disability" measure contained in the CPS for drawing conclusions about the overall experience of the disabled or the effectiveness of the ADA. Some argue that requiring a disability to be "work limiting" can be too narrow (Kruse and Schur 2002; McNeil 2000). Others contend that not appropriately defining what a work-limiting disability is results in too broad of an inclusion of respondents (Hale 2001 and Kirchner 1996). Yet, others provide evidence supporting the representative nature of the CPS for monitoring outcomes among the disabled (Burkhauser, Daly, and Houtenville 2001). It is because of this controversy that confirmatory evidence of the CPS results is sought from an additional data source. Regardless, the reader should be aware that this book makes use of "work-limiting disability" as the identifier of a disabled person. In addition, it is expected that when focusing on labor market outcomes, those who report a work-limiting disability are the most likely to feel the greatest impacts of the ADA, should they exist.

Table 1.1 reports the potential sample sizes for each year obtained from the CPS. Actual sample sizes for each analysis may differ because of missing data or the use of specific subsamples (e.g., the unemployed only).[6] While the sample sizes vary somewhat from year to year, the proportion of disabled to nondisabled remains fairly constant, and most analyses benefit from roughly 1,500 disabled workers and 50,000 nondisabled workers.

Table 1.1 Sample Sizes for Merged CPS Data Files

Year	Total	Disabled			Nondisabled		
		All	Labor force participants	Employed	All	Labor force participants	Employed
1981	100,291	9,818	2,022	1,744	90,473	60,873	56,656
1982	94,351	9,617	1,962	1,661	84,734	57,006	52,015
1983	93,720	9,119	1,788	1,490	84,601	56,606	51,114
1984	94,683	9,654	1,922	1,661	85,029	57,591	53,507
1985	95,075	9,832	1,931	1,648	85,243	58,111	54,192
1986	90,341	8,931	1,848	1,581	81,410	55,604	51,935
1987	88,507	8,513	1,805	1,560	79,994	54,829	51,591
1988	85,371	7,811	1,697	1,493	77,560	52,258	49,625
1989	85,224	7,913	1,713	1,533	77,311	53,364	50,789
1990	93,625	8,745	1,919	1,692	84,880	58,896	56,005
1991	92,958	8,681	1,833	1,598	84,277	58,172	54,558
1992	90,520	8,547	1,913	1,614	81,973	56,617	52,779
1993	90,056	8,842	1,950	1,684	81,214	55,926	52,316
1994	88,674	9,709	1,810	1,602	78,965	55,341	52,246
1995	77,674	8,654	1,507	1,336	69,020	48,217	45,775
1996	77,188	8,396	1,535	1,379	68,792	48,356	45,892
1997	78,322	8,418	1,609	1,456	69,904	49,437	47,112
1998	77,583	7,796	1,468	1,332	69,787	49,403	47,370
1999	77,487	7,625	1,392	1,266	69,862	49,406	47,542
2000	79,242	7,917	1,488	1,358	71,325	50,825	48,999

Since the ADA (and similar legislation) was designed to improve the labor market conditions of a group of workers, the analyses presented here will be almost purely cross-sectional. The result is a comprehensive comparison of the labor market experiences of one group of workers (the disabled) with that of another group of workers (the nondisabled). When making comparisons across groups of people, there will surely always be exceptions to the norm. It is important to recognize, however, that policy is rarely designed around exceptions. The use of individual data in the analyses does allow for control of identifiable individual characteristics (other than the group-defining characteristic of being disabled) in the determination of workers' experiences. The premise, of course, is that identical disabled and nondisabled workers should have the same labor market experience. This presupposition, which holds in making any comparisons across groups of workers (i.e., men versus women, or blacks versus whites), is more problematic in making comparisons across disability status; there are likely more unobservable characteristics across disability status than, for example, across gender. In addition, since most of the analyses consider the experience of those in the labor market, or at least control for selection into the labor market, no restriction is imposed on age.[7]

For each of the analyses, it is important to distinguish any changes in outcomes that might have resulted from the enactment of the ADA from any long-term trend. In other words, changes in the labor market experiences of workers with disabilities may reflect an evolving social awareness that culminated in the passage of the ADA, rather than the other way around. Consequently, this book documents labor market outcomes from 1981 through 2000.[8] In addition, since a major overhaul of the CPS questionnaire was undertaken in 1994, care is taken to differentiate any ADA impact from a potential statistical artifact (see Polivka 1996).

Also, due to the complicated matching across one to four months of the CPS, all analyses have been performed unweighted. According to Wooldridge (1999), "stratification based on exogenous variables does not cause any problems: estimators that ignore the stratification are consistent and asymptotically normal, and the usual variance matrix estimators are consistent" (p. 1386). Since stratification in the CPS sampling design is based on exogenous variables (geographic and demographic), and the attrition that results from the matching procedure is likely unsystematic, weights should be unnecessary (for further evidence on this point, see DuMouchel and Duncan 1983; Manski and McFadden 1981). In addition, any effect of stratification on the estimation can be accounted for by including indicator variables that correspond to the strata (Ginther and Hayes 2001), so demographic variables (such as disability status) should control for any observable effect sampling based on those characteristics might have (either initially or through attrition of matching). Any systematic attrition or sample loss due to unobservables will not be accounted for, but also cannot be corrected using weights.

DISABLED AMERICANS

As a first look at the data used for the analyses in the following chapters, Figure 1.1 depicts the percentage of the sample in each year and the percentage of workers in each year indicating a work-limiting disability.[9] The vertical lines correspond to the phase-in years of the ADA. It is of interest to know whether there is any noticeable change

Figure 1.1 Percentage of Sample and of Workers in the CPS Data Set Indicating a Work-Limiting Disability, 1981–2000

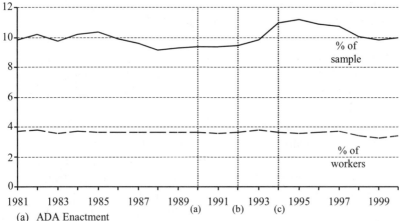

(a) ADA Enactment
(b) ADA Phase I
(c) ADA Phase II

in the reporting of having a work-limiting disability, particularly on the part of workers.

Over the time period from 1981 to 2000, an average of 10 percent of the entire sample indicated having a work-limiting disability.[10] There is a significant 1 percentage point difference between the averages prior to and including 1991, and 1994 and later.[11] Kreider (1999) finds evidence of substantial overreporting of limitations by nonworkers, a behavior which may be enhanced in the presence of protective legislation. It has also been found that the passage of the Personal Responsibility and Work Opportunity Reconciliation Act (PRWORA) in 1996, which essentially put a time limit on welfare payments, resulted in a movement of qualified recipients from the welfare rolls to SSI (Lewin Group 1999). The Lewin Group found "a very substantial flow of program participants from AFDC to SSI during the pre-reform period" (p. ES-3). The "pre-reform" period would coincide with the rise in the percentage reporting being disabled between 1993 and 1995 in Figure 1.1. However, the percentage has been declining fairly steadily since 1995. This issue of increased reporting of a work-limiting disability among the entire population is taken up in greater detail in Chapter 2, and again points to the potential endogeneity problems inherent in using a self-reported disability classification.

The proportion of *workers* indicating a work-limiting disability has remained fairly constant at about 3 percent across the entire time span; there is no significant difference in the 1981–1991 and 1994–2000 periods. So, while heightened awareness of the ADA and other program changes may have increased the reporting of work-limiting disabilities among the population, the primary individuals of focus for this study, i.e., workers, do not seem to have changed their reporting behavior in a way that might be expected to bias the analysis. In addition, given that the reporting percentage of the population has begun to decline again, and that the share of workers seems unaffected, it is safe to say that CPS survey design changes that occurred in 1994 do not seem to have impacted the reporting of those with work-limiting disabilities.

Comparing raw averages of disabled and nondisabled workers across the time period, one can see that there are some significant demographic differences among these categories of workers. Table 1.2 reports averages across time for a variety of demographics for disabled

Table 1.2 Means of Select Demographic Variables for Disabled and Nondisabled Workers over Entire Time Period, CPS, 1981–2000

Variable	Disabled workers	Nondisabled workers
Hours of work	33.97	38.01
Female = 1	0.47	0.48
Single = 1	0.48	0.40
Nonwhite = 1	0.13	0.13
College degree = 1[a]	0.10	0.18
Midwest = 1	0.26	0.25
South = 1	0.29	0.30
West = 1	0.24	0.22
Norteast = 1	0.21	0.23
Age	43.43	37.49

[a] Coding of education changed substantially in 1992; these averages reflect the average across years 1992–2000.

and nondisabled workers. The distribution of workers across occupations and industries is of interest, as well, but that will be explored in great detail in Chapter 4. While females and nonwhites seem to be equally represented among disabled and nondisabled workers, and each group of workers appears to be equally distributed geographically, there are some notable differences in demographics. Disabled workers, on average, work fewer hours, are less likely to have a college degree, are older, and are more likely to be single. While means across time give us some idea of the relative differences between worker categories, they tell us nothing about trends.

One trend of particular interest is the change in average hours per week over time among workers. Figure 1.2 depicts the average hours of disabled and nondisabled workers for each year between 1981 and 2000. While the average weekly hours of nondisabled workers rise fairly steadily over this time period from 37.5 in 1981 to 38.7 in 2000, the hours of disabled workers fall from an average of 34.7 in 1981 to 33.8 in 2000. Since a dramatic part of this decline occurred after 1992, one might suggest that the ADA was a factor. Full-time jobs may be less available to disabled workers; the ADA may have induced employers to be more flexible regarding hours of work in accommodating a worker's disability; or workers with more serious disabilities, unable to work full-time, may have begun to enter the labor market (Kaye

**Figure 1.2 Average Weekly Hours of Disabled and Nondisabled Workers,
CPS, 1981–2000**

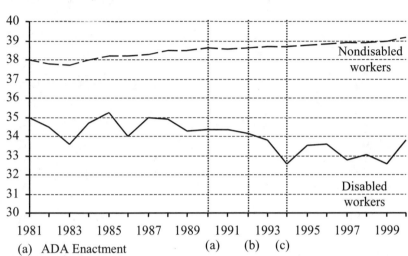

(a) ADA Enactment
(b) ADA Phase I
(c) ADA Phase II

2002). Issues related to differences in part-time employment across disability status will be evaluated in greater detail in Chapter 4.

SURVEY OF INCOME AND PROGRAM PARTICIPATION (SIPP)

Data from the SIPP were used to construct a sample to supplement the analyses from the CPS. The goal in employing the SIPP is twofold. First, it provides validation of the results obtained using the CPS. Second, given that the SIPP allows identification of the nature of a respondent's disability, some questions regarding the importance of the type of disability can be addressed. The samples from the SIPP have been constructed to match those from the CPS as closely as possible (e.g., regarding variable definitions, etc.).[12] While providing more detail related to the respondent's disability, the SIPP does not provide as long or as large a data set with which to study labor market experience. Table 1.3 provides sample size details for the SIPP samples constructed

Table 1.3 Sample Sizes for SIPP Data Files

Year	Total	Disabled			Nondisabled		
		All	Labor force participants	Employed	All	Labor force participants	Employed
1986	18,290	2,102	759	650	16,188	12,036	11,191
1987	33,884	3,939	1,470	1,297	29,945	22,278	20,932
1988	34,284	3,995	1,476	1,324	30,289	22,623	21,579
1989	16,274	1,826	651	579	14,448	10,949	10,505
1990	34,010	3,788	1,404	1,233	30,222	22,771	21,629
1991	51,140	5,596	1,998	1,755	45,544	34,392	32,328
1992	76,496	8,231	2,936	2,570	68,265	52,105	48,582
1993	73,831	8,112	2,839	2,442	65,719	49,861	46,694
1994	50,384	5,495	1,881	1,680	44,889	34,338	32,529
1995	23,753	2,610	918	829	21,143	16,313	15,550
1996	57,625	5,865	2,049	1,871	51,760	41,158	39,357
1997	46,914	4,706	1,584	1,470	42,208	33,718	32,558

for each year. Due to the sampling structure of the SIPP, the sample sizes varied from just over 16,000 to over 76,000. However, as Figure 1.3 illustrates, the representation of the disabled within the whole sample and within the working subsample has remained consistent, although slightly declining over the period.[13] In addition, there does not seem to be any shift in the trends during the ADA phase-in period.

The percentages of the sample and of workers indicating a work-limiting disability are slightly higher in the SIPP than in the CPS. This occurs for two reasons. SIPP respondents are given two opportunities to answer a disability question positively. In addition, since the sample came from Wave 2 (the second survey within a panel), the respondent is reminded if he or she indicated a disability in Wave 1 (the first survey), increasing the chances for a positive response (also see Kruse and Schur 2002). The percentages reflected in Figure 1.3 are consistent with those found by other researchers using the SIPP (e.g., DeLeire 2000; Kruse and Schur 2002).

The nature of a person's disability is placed into one of 30 different categories (including "other"). In order to be able to include controls for type of disability, these categories were combined to correspond to the groupings used by the Social Security Administration.[14] Aggregation was necessary due to category size limitations; the four groups included as controls were: 1) musculoskeletal systems and special

**Figure 1.3 Percentage of Sample and of Workers in the SIPP Data Set
Indicating a Work-Limiting Disability, 1986–1997**

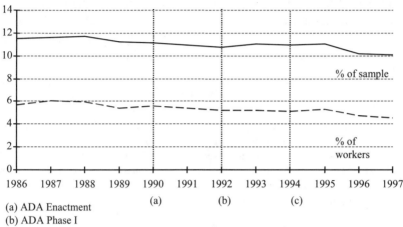

(a) ADA Enactment
(b) ADA Phase I
(c) ADA Phase II

senses; 2) internal systems; 3) neurological systems and mental disorders; and 4) other. Figure 1.4 presents the distribution of all disabled individuals and disabled workers across these categorizations. The largest group by type of disability contains those with musculoskeletal and special senses disabilities; the internal systems category is generally the next largest, followed by neurological and mental disorders (typically), and other. One can observe a slight upward trend in the

**Figure 1.4 Distribution of Disabled Individuals across Disability Type,
SIPP, 1986–1997**

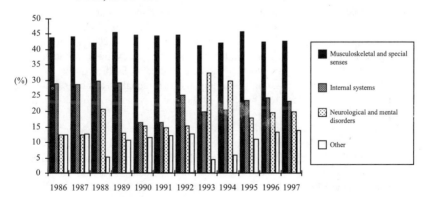

neurological and mental disorders classification, while the proportion for internal systems has declined slightly, and that for musculoskeletal and special senses has remained fairly consistent over the time period. These four classifications will be used to determine whether the labor market experience varies across type of disability, an important consideration when trying to mold policy to impact those most affected.

Notes

1. Further details of the history and provision of the Rehabilitation Act of 1973 can be found in Ellner and Bender (1980).
2. See Advisory Commission on Intergovernmental Relations (1989).
3. Data provided by the Roper Center for Public Opinion Research, University of Connecticut, Storrs, Connecticut. By 1999, 67 percent of those surveyed by the same polling group *had* heard of the ADA.
4. This issue has often been raised by historians. For example, see Landes and Solmon (1972). Donohue and Heckman (1991) also empirically address the subject with regard to civil rights legislation. They conclude that federal civil rights legislation did play a major role in the progress of blacks beginning in 1965.
5. Some have even suggested that our analyses of the labor market impact of the ADA are misguided, and that attempts to quantify an impact in the labor market are merely arrogant efforts to justify our assumptions about how the labor market should operate (see Schwochau and Blanck 2000).
6. Appendix A contains additional information pertaining to the matching and merging of the CPS files across months and concerning other details learned in the process.
7. The exceptions are analyses of employment where age is restricted to 15–65 years.
8. Prior to 1981, identification of a disability in the CPS was made only in the context of why a respondent was not working.
9. See Table C.1, in Appendix C, for percentages used to generate Figure 1.1.
10. The percentages of the entire sample that are disabled are slightly higher than those reported by Burkhauser, Daly, and Houtenville (2000, 2001). This is likely the result of the matching technique employed here, allowing for a much larger sample, and thus greater opportunity to be classified as disabled.
11. The Z statistic corresponding to the hypothesis of equal means over these time periods is 3.18, leading to a rejection of the null hypothesis of equality at the 99 percent confidence level.
12. Details of the construction of the SIPP samples are contained in Appendix B.
13. There are two check variables in the topical module used to identify a work-limiting disability for the 1986–1993 panels. The 1996 panel has only one check variable, which may explain the slightly lower incidence of a work-limiting disability in the 1996 and 1997 SIPP samples. Kruse and Schur (2002) make use of

the functional limitations module (rather than the work disability module used here) and note a similar decline in disability percentages in later years due to question placement in that module. These nuances in the survey design among panels are clearly important and raise, once again, the concerns associated with using a self-reported disability indicator.

14. The Social Security Administration's listing of impairments for disability status purposes can be found on the Internet at <http://www.ssa.gov/OP_Home/cfr20/404/404-ap09.htm>. The mental disorder category does include those classified as mentally retarded. The mentally retarded group is not broken out into a separate category in order to be consistent with the classification used by the Social Security Administration, to correspond with the groupings used by others (e.g., DeLeire 2000; Kruse and Schur 2002), and to preserve reasonable sample sizes within the categories. The employment and wage analyses were reestimated with mental retardation as a separate category, and none of the results or conclusions changed.

2
Employment
(Co-authored with Ludmila Rovba)

Employment levels of the disabled are affected by both labor supply and labor demand issues. Individuals suffering from a functional disability will also experience a larger cost to entering the labor market as, holding all else constant, greater effort or sacrifices must be made relative to nondisabled workers. The net result is that the reservation wage (the wage at which a person is willing to enter the labor market) for disabled individuals will be higher than for the nondisabled, and fewer disabled people will choose to enter the labor market, *ceteris paribus*. In addition, a person's functional disability will be more likely to render him or her less productive than an otherwise identical, nondisabled person. Consequently, the disabled worker will be less likely to qualify for a given job and therefore less likely to be hired. Merely a perception of lower productivity or a greater difficulty of predicting a disabled worker's productivity will reduce the likelihood of the individual being hired. So, for both supply and demand reasons, the employment levels of disabled workers would be expected to be lower than those of nondisabled workers.[1] Figure 2.1 presents evidence from the CPS consistent with this prediction.[2] The proportion of disabled individuals employed in any given year is at least 44 percentage points lower than the share of nondisabled individuals employed in that year. Other observations are worth mentioning in comparing employment percentages. The recession dips of the early 1980s and early 1990s are obvious for the nondisabled, but not nearly as severe (in percentage terms) for the disabled. In addition, the employment percentage for the nondisabled has made a fairly steady climb over the entire period compared with the relatively stagnant, then declining, employment percentage of the disabled.

Legislation that potentially affects the costs of either labor force participation or of hiring a group of workers can be expected to impact the employment levels of that group. The ADA, through its required

21

**Figure 2.1 Percentage Employed of Disabled and Nondisabled
Individuals, CPS, 1981–2000**

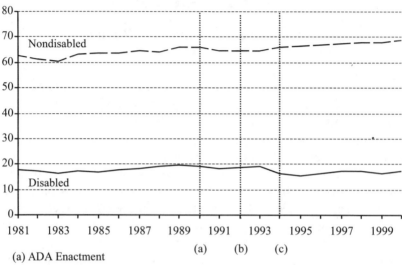

(a) ADA Enactment
(b) ADA Phase I
(c) ADA Phase II

NOTE: Individuals in this figure refer to all people, regardless of labor force participation status.

accommodations, can be anticipated to reduce the cost to a disabled individual of entering the labor force, thus promoting labor force participation.[3] It might also be argued that greater accommodation of a disabled worker's limitations will result in enhanced productivity of that disabled worker, thus increasing the likelihood of employment. (This will be the case, however, only if employers are able to accurately predict the cost and productivity gains of such accommodations.) If those required accommodations, however, are "binding" in the sense that the employer would not undertake them in the absence of the ADA, it must be the case that increased productivity of the disabled worker does not offset the cost of implementing those accommodations.[4] In other words, the value of the productivity gains is not as great as the cost of accommodation. This may result in decreased employment probabilities of disabled workers, since the cost of hiring a disabled worker has increased. Referring back to Figure 2.1, there does not seem to be any noticeable, or permanent, change in the employment percentages for disabled workers around the time of passage of the ADA, although there is a slight drop around the second phase-in period. This chapter explores more fully the employment probabilities of disabled and nondisabled workers between 1981 and 2000, controlling for observable individual characteristics and labor force participation.

The issue of joint versus unconditional employment differences is explored through estimating a bivariate probit model, controlling for selection into the labor market. This is followed by an examination of how employment has changed across size of firm. The analyses indicate that, *at worst*, employment probabilities of disabled workers have not deteriorated relative to nondisabled workers, and that employment of disabled workers has shifted from medium and small firms to large firms.

UNCONDITIONAL AND JOINT PROBABILITIES

The labor market provisions of the ADA were motivated by a desire to eliminate barriers to disabled individuals that might exist in the labor market. An appropriate assessment of the success of the ADA in this endeavor would involve evaluation of unconditional employment outcomes. In other words, the question to be answered is whether there has been any progress in employment outcomes for the disabled person drawn from random, controlling for the likelihood that he or she is a labor force participant. The resulting probability of interest is an unconditional probability of employment. An alternative question, which has been the source of recent condemnation of the employment impacts of the ADA, is whether there has been any progress in employment among *all* disabled people. This second question involves evaluation of a joint outcome: what is the probability of entering the labor force *and* being employed? While the impact of the ADA on labor force participation may be of interest from a social, resource, and demographic perspective, the unconditional probability will tell us more about the barriers disabled *workers* face, which is the focus of the employment provisions of the ADA. Consideration of the joint outcome (or, employment among all disabled people) confounds conclusions regarding the employment impact of the ADA with labor supply decisions.

When considering the unconditional probability, one must control for unobservable characteristics that might both affect the labor force participation decision and the employment outcome. Without controlling for this potential self-selection, any differences measured in the employment probabilities may actually be confounded by variations between characteristics that affect the labor supply decision of disabled and nondisabled persons. If these characteristics change in a systematic way over time, the problem is magnified. A bivariate probit model with selection will be estimated in order to obtain information on unconditional employment outcomes and to control for selection into the labor market at the same time. The bivariate specification allows for the two outcomes (labor force participation and employment) to be impacted by the same unobservable factors (e.g., motivation). The selectivity part of the model is merely a recognition that we do not get to see the employment outcome unless the person is in the labor market to begin with, and that those we observe in the labor market may have systematically different employment outcomes than those not in the labor market. Correcting for selectivity allows us to make inferences for *anyone* from the population, not just those found in the labor market; this is what makes the probability unconditional.[5]

The following model defines the relationship assumed between labor force participation of person i (LFP$_i$), employment (EMP$_i$), and individual characteristics that are believed to affect the labor force participation decision (X_{1i}) and the employment outcome (X_{2i}):

$$(2.1) \quad \text{LFP}_i = \alpha_1 + \gamma_1'X_{1i} + \beta_1 \text{DISABLE}_i + \epsilon_{1i}$$
$$= \begin{cases} 1 \text{ if person } i \text{ is in the labor force} \\ 0 \text{ otherwise} \end{cases}$$

$$(2.2) \quad \text{EMP}_i = \alpha_2 + \gamma_2'X_{2i} + \beta_2 \text{DISABLE}_i + \epsilon_{2i}$$
$$= \begin{cases} 1 \text{ if person } i \text{ is employed} \\ 0 \text{ otherwise} \end{cases}$$

DISABLE$_i$ is equal to 1 if person i is disabled, 0 otherwise, and ϵ_{1i} and ϵ_{2i} are distributed as a bivariate normal with means equal to 0, variances equal to 1, and correlation equal to ρ. In addition, of course, EMP$_i$ is only observed if LFP$_i$ = 1.[6] X_{1i} and X_{2i} both include age; age squared; female, nonwhite, education, and regional dummies; and state unemployment rate. The labor force participation equation regressors (X_{1i}) also include nonlabor income, marital status, and a worked-last-year indicator. The employment equation regressors (X_{2i}) also include number of weeks worked last year. The impact of having a work-limiting disability on employment, then, is determined by calculating the probability of interest for each person (using the estimated parameter coefficients, α_1, α_2, γ_1, γ_2, β_1, and β_2), varying the disability index between 0 and 1, then averaging the difference across the sample.[7] The model is estimated for each year separately, and the marginal impact of having a work-limiting disability is calculated.[8] The significance of having a work-limiting disability is determined from the significance of the estimated coefficient. Figure 2.2 reflects the marginal effect of having a work-limiting disability on the predicted joint probability of labor force participation and employment in each year.[9]

The impact of having a work-limiting disability on the joint labor force and employment probability intensifies (becomes more negative), rather dramatically, in 1994, corresponding to the second phase of the ADA. The marginal effect increases from an average of −15 percentage points prior to 1994 to an average of −19 percentage points

Figure 2.2 Impact of Disability on Joint Labor Force Participation and Employment Probabilities, CPS, 1981–2000

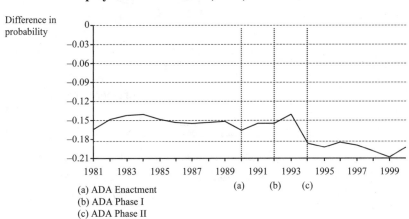

(a) ADA Enactment
(b) ADA Phase I
(c) ADA Phase II

between 1994 and 2000. In other words, having a work-limiting disability decreased an individual's joint probability of being in the labor force and employed by 4 percentage points *more* after 1994 than it did prior to 1994. This dramatic relative decline in the joint probability for the disabled is the result on which DeLeire (2000) and Acemoglu and Angrist (2001) base their warnings regarding the ADA.

Breaking the joint probability into its employment and labor force participation components, it becomes clear that this salient change in 1994 is driven by decreases in labor force participation among the disabled. Figure 2.3 plots the predicted (unconditional) employment and labor force participation probabilities for the disabled alone using the same parameter estimates that generated Figure 2.2. After increasing fairly steadily, the predicted labor force participation rate declines in 1994 and stays below 1986 levels. At the same time, and with the exception of the recession years of 1991–1993, the predicted unconditional employment probability among the disabled has increased fairly steadily.

Figure 2.3 Separate Predictions of Employment and Labor Force Participation Probabilities for the Disabled, CPS, 1987–2000

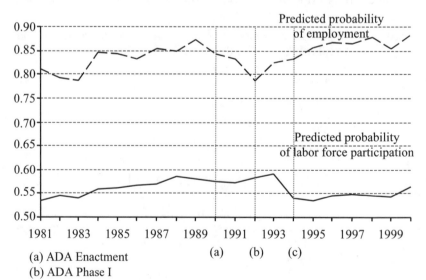

(a) ADA Enactment
(b) ADA Phase I
(c) ADA Phase II

Again, in evaluating the barriers facing disabled workers, change in the unconditional employment probability is a more appropriate measure than the change in the joint labor force and employment outcome. Consequently, the condemnation of the employment impact of the ADA by DeLeire (2000) and Acemoglu and Angrist (2001) is misplaced, since both of these analyses confound their evaluation of employment changes with changes in labor supply decisions. The results in Figure 2.3 show that the decline in employment probabilities among all disabled people is labor-supply driven and does not reflect an increase in employment barriers for individuals with disabilities. One may argue that the disabled have decreased their labor supply behavior in response to a real or perceived change in employment probabilities (demonstrating a potential "feedback effect"), but the predicted unconditional employment probabilities are not consistent with this view.[10]

It may be the case, however, that the condemnation of the ADA by recent studies should be aimed at its apparent impact on labor force participation. For example, if the ADA resulted in lower wages for the disabled (their employment has now become more expensive through required accommodations), it is possible that the wage would fall below the reservation wage of a significant number of disabled labor force participants, causing them to drop out of the labor market. It may also be the case that the severity of disabilities has been growing over time, resulting in declining labor force participation rates (Kaye 2002). The next section explores this drop in labor force participation rates among the disabled in greater detail.

EXPLAINING THE DECLINE IN LABOR FORCE PARTICIPATION RATES

Even if the ADA has not had a negative employment impact but has inadvertently discouraged the disabled from seeking employment, there would be a concern worthy of further policy consideration. The disabled and nondisabled populations can be represented in the following chart:

	In labor force	Not in labor force
Nondisabled	A	B
Disabled	C	D

Cells A through D contain a given number of people at any given time period. A decrease in the disabled labor force participation rate (LFPR_d) corresponds to a decline in the ratio $C/(C+D)$. This ratio can decline if C decreases and/or if D increases.[11] If C falls, these people must go somewhere; it is most likely that they either go to A (stay in the labor force but change their identification to nondisabled), or go to D (keep their identification as disabled, but leave the labor force). It is this latter possibility that is of potential concern. Although the ADA was not designed as a policy to necessarily increase the labor force participation rate among the disabled, a precipitous drop in such participation, even remotely attributable to the ADA, is considered by many as undesirable. The LFPR_d may also fall, however, as a result of an increase in D. Again, the increase in D must come from somewhere; the most likely candidates are C (disabled leaving the labor force) or B (nondisabled, nonparticipants in the labor force changing their identity to disabled). The latter (movement from B to D) is what might result, for example, from a shift of (nonparticipant) welfare recipients away from welfare programs and into disability programs; this movement following the reform of welfare has been documented (the Lewin Group 1999; also see Davies, Iams, and Rupp 2000). Greater effort to be classified (and identified) as disabled might also result from increased generosity of the disability programs themselves (see Autor and Duggan 2001; Bound and Waidmann 2002).[12] This could be consistent with the finding by Kreider (1999) that nonworkers substantially overreport a work limitation.

So, the question is, which is it? Are the disabled moving out of the labor force (from C to D) or are more nonparticipants identifying themselves as disabled (from B to D)? One way to get an indication of the movement across these cells is to evaluate the trends in the percentages represented in each cell. These results are depicted in the following chart. The percentage in each cell represents the growth, or decline, experienced within that cell. The cells exhaust the population, so the changes sum to zero.[13]

	In labor force	Not in labor force
Nondisabled	+0.1504** (A)	−0.2309** (B)
Disabled	−0.0225** (C)	+0.1030* (D)

** = significant at the 95 percent confidence level.
* = significant at the 90 percent confidence level.

The largest net change in the cells was movement of the nondisabled out of the nonparticipant category (cell B). The coefficient indicates that the nondisabled, nonparticipant percentage declined an average of about 0.23 percentage points per year between 1990 and 2000. Even if the entire increase in cell A (nondisabled labor force participants) came from cell B, that still means that the overwhelming bulk of the increase in cell D (disabled nonparticipants) came from cell B as well, not cell C. In fact, the smallest net cell change was among the disabled labor force participants. This result provides strong evidence that the observed decline in the $LFPR_d$ was not the result of the disabled fleeing the labor force but was most likely due to the reidentification of some nonparticipants from nondisabled to disabled (movement from B to D). While providing an explanation for the decline in $LFPR_d$, this movement from cell B to cell D is a reminder of the criticism of using self-reported disability status in statistical analyses. This also suggests that endogeneity will be less of a concern for analyses that focus exclusively on labor force participants in evaluating the labor market experience of the disabled (using a self-reported measure of disability). In other words, there is less movement across disability status among labor market participants than among nonparticipants. In addition, these results indicate that the observed decline in the $LFPR_d$ should not be considered as casting a shadow on the measured impacts of the ADA on employment.

POOLED, CROSS-SECTIONAL ANALYSIS

Along with cross-sectional analyses, an analysis across time is performed to help quantify any difference in predicted probabilities of employment between disabled and nondisabled individuals after the ADA relative to before the ADA. The strategy used to accomplish this is to estimate a cross-sectional, time-series bivariate probit model with dummy variables representing whether the observation shows up in the data pre-ADA or post-ADA and whether the observation is a disabled or nondisabled person. These dummy variables are also interacted to determine whether being disabled had any greater impact on employment after the ADA than before the ADA, relative to the experience of a nondisabled person.[14] While this type of pooled, cross-sectional analysis has been applied by many researchers (for example, Card 1992; Gruber 1994 and 1996; Zveglich and Rodgers 1996; and Hamermesh and Trejo 2000), the technique also has its critics (such as Heckman 1996). The primary criticism of this approach is that it is impossible to control for unobserved changes in the environment that occurred at the same time as the event of interest. For example, the second phase of the ADA occurred in 1994. This was also when the CPS underwent a major overhaul, and there is no way to disentangle these two events. In addition, the economy began its longest-running expansion in recent history at the same time that the ADA was being phased in, which could potentially confound any measurable impact of the ADA through this estimation strategy. One advantage of the analysis here is that the CPS survey changes should not have a differential impact on the disabled and nondisabled (as the changes did not affect measurement or classification by disability),[15] and general business cycle activity should essentially impact the disabled and nondisabled in relatively the same proportions.[16] Nonetheless, the state unemployment rate is included as a regressor in order to capture any general business cycle influences.

The empirical model looks just like the bivariate probit with selection estimated in one year, except with the additional time-period dummy variables:

$$(2.3) \quad \text{LFP}_i = \alpha_1 + \gamma_1'X_{1i} + \beta_1\text{DISABLE}_i + \phi_1\text{POST}_i$$
$$+ \theta_1\text{DISABLE}_i \times \text{POST}_i + \epsilon_{1i}$$

(2.4) $\text{EMP}_i = \alpha_2 + \gamma_2'X_{2i} + \beta_2\text{DISABLE}_i + \phi_2\text{POST}_i$
$+ \theta_2\text{DISABLE}_i \times \text{POST}_i + \epsilon_{2i}.$

Again, $\text{LFP}_i = 1$ if person i is in the labor force, 0 otherwise, and EMP_i is not observed unless $\text{LFP}_i = 1$. DISABLE_i is equal to 1 if person i is disabled, 0 otherwise; POST_i is equal to 1 if person i is observed in 1992 or later; X_{1i} and X_{2i} include individual demographic characteristics; and ϵ_{1i} and ϵ_{2i} are distributed as a bivariate normal with means equal to 0, variances equal to 1, and correlation equal to ρ.

In this framework, the affected group (the disabled) is controlled for by a dummy variable indicating whether the individual has a work-limiting disability (DISABLE), and the time period is controlled for by a dummy variable indicating whether the ADA had been implemented yet or not (POST); ϕ_1 and ϕ_2 are the estimated parameter coefficients for the time-period dummies. Given the nonlinearity of the bivariate probit estimation procedure, a single parameter coefficient does not tell us the additional impact the ADA had on the difference in employment probabilities between the disabled and nondisabled. The difference in the impact of having a work-limiting disability on employment across the two time periods can be calculated by evaluating the probabilities of interest for each person, varying the DISABLE and POST dummy variables, then taking the difference between these probabilities, and averaging this difference across the sample.[17] The significance of the coefficient on the interacted DISABLE $\times$ POST (θ_1, and θ_2) will, however, yield significance levels of the calculated marginal effects.

The decision of when one would expect the ADA to have its strongest impact (i.e., how to define POST) is debatable. One might expect some impact when the ADA was enacted (1990). However, employers were not required to respond until 1992 (for employers with 25 or more employees) and 1994 (for employers with 15 or more employees). The year 1992 was chosen for defining POST since that is the first year of enforcement of the law. Table 2.1 details the regression results.

The coefficients on DISABLE $\times$ POST presented in Table 2.1 are consistent with the conclusions drawn from Figure 2.2. Namely, labor force participation among the disabled declined significantly after implementation of the ADA, relative to labor force participation among the nondisabled. In addition, while all other regressors contribute significantly to explaining employment (all at the 99 percent confidence

Table 2.1 Labor Force Participation and Employment Bivariate Probit with Selection Results, CPS, Combined Years 1981–2000

Regressor	Labor force participation equation	Employment equation
Intercept	−2.9988***	0.6421***
	(0.0152)	(0.0215)
Age (00)	13.3928***	−1.3265***
	(0.0742)	(0.1176)
Age^2 (0000)	−16.6844***	2.2159***
	(0.0905)	(0.1544)
Female = 1	−0.4651***	0.1811***
	(0.0032)	(0.0047)
Nonwhite = 1	−0.0176***	−0.2393***
	(0.0045)	(0.0058)
High school grad = 1	0.2094***	0.0762***
	(0.0041)	(0.0061)
Some college = 1	0.1127***	0.2076***
	(0.0046)	(0.0067)
College grad = 1	0.2754***	0.3730***
	(0.0053)	(0.0083)
Advanced degree = 1	0.3378***	0.3479***
	(0.0082)	(0.0134)
Central city = 1	0.0398***	−0.0321***
	(0.0051)	(0.0070)
Midwest = 1	0.0530***	0.0337***
	(0.0045)	(0.0065)
South = 1	0.0196***	0.0813***
	(0.0042)	(0.0064)
West = 1	−0.0233	0.0218***
	(0.0046)	(0.0067)
Single household = 1	0.2148***	—
	(0.0036)	
Nonlabor income (000000)	−16.6473***	—
	(0.2922)	
Worked last year = 1	2.0763***	—
	(0.0035)	
Weeks worked last year (00)	—	3.2187***
		(0.0151)
State unemployment rate (0)	−0.0901***	−0.6357***
	(0.0076)	(0.0103)
DISABLE = 1	−0.7624***	−0.2012***
	(0.0080)	(0.0143)

Table 2.1 (continued)

Regressor	Labor force participation equation		Employment equation
POST (year = 1992 or later) = 1	0.0677***		−0.0139***
	(0.0035)		(0.0051)
DISABLE × POST = 1	−0.1706***		−0.0298
	(0.0120)		(0.0225)
Rho		0.0371***	
		(0.0065)	
Log-likelihood		−596,816	
Number of observations		1,359,885	

NOTE: Standard errors are in parentheses.
*** = significant at the 99 percent confidence level. Notation of, for example, (00) indicates regressor has been scaled by dividing by 100.

level), being disabled after ADA implementation is not one of them; the disabled are no more or less likely to be employed than the nondisabled, post-ADA relative to pre-ADA. In other words, the ADA has not changed the relative employment probability between disabled and nondisabled workers.[18]

Table 2.2 translates the parameter coefficients in Table 2.1 into marginal effects. These marginal effects indicate that the employment probability of disabled labor force participants, relative to nondisabled labor force participants, declines *at most* 0.6 of a percentage point post-

Table 2.2 Change in Marginal Effect of Disability on Labor Force Participation and Employment Probabilities

	Probability (LFP = 1)		Probability (EMP = 1)		Probability (EMP = 1, LFP = 1)	
	Before ADA	After ADA	Before ADA	After ADA	Before ADA	After ADA
Nondisabled	0.7284	0.7397	0.8592	0.8569	0.6718	0.6798
Disabled	0.5693	0.5431	0.8233	0.8148	0.5202	0.4942
Marginal effect	−0.1591	−0.1966	−0.0359	−0.0421	−0.1516	−0.1856
Change in marginal effect	−0.0375		−0.0062		−0.0340	

NOTE: Probabilities calculated using parameter coefficients from Table 2.1.

ADA (see column 2, last row). However, this effect is not significantly different from zero; in a model where all other coefficients are significantly different from zero, this is notable. On the other hand, the labor force participation rate declined significantly, by nearly 4 percentage points more for the disabled than for the nondisabled, post-ADA.[19]

EVIDENCE FROM THE SIPP

The analysis detailed in Equations 2.3 and 2.4 is reestimated using the sample obtained from the SIPP for the years 1986 through 1997. Table 2.3 reports the coefficients of interest from estimating the bivariate probit model with selection using the SIPP data. The results reported in Table 2.3 mirror those in Table 2.1, with one difference: employment among the disabled *increased more* post- versus pre-ADA than did the employment of the nondisabled. This positive 0.0768 coefficient on DISABLE × POST translates into a 0.8 of a percentage point higher employment probability for the disabled relative to the

Table 2.3 Labor Force Participation and Employment Bivariate Probit with Selection Results, SIPP Combined Years 1986–1997

Regressor	Labor force participation equation	Employment equation
DISABLE = 1	−0.9404***	−0.2435***
	(0.0105)	(0.0211)
POST (year = 1992 or later) = 1	0.0293***	−0.0348***
	(0.0048)	(0.0077)
DISABLE × POST = 1	−0.1360***	0.0768***
	(0.0129)	(0.0250)
Rho		−0.4811***
		(0.0204)
Log-likelihood		−292,341
Number of observations		500,560

NOTE: Additional regressors included age; age squared; state unemployment rate; female, nonwhite, education, regional dummy variables; an indicator for SMSA residence (employment); and non-labor income and marital status (labor force participation). Standard errors are in parentheses.

*** = significant at the 99 percent confidence level.

nondisabled. In addition, the relative decline in labor force participation among the disabled found in the CPS data is also seen using the SIPP data as well.

Along with the reestimation of Equations 2.3 and 2.4, a specification is estimated in which the impact of having a disability post-ADA is allowed to vary by type of impairment:[20]

(2.5) $\begin{aligned} \text{LFP}_i = {} & \alpha_1 + \gamma_1'X_{1i} + \beta_1^S \text{ MUSCULOSKELETAL}_i + \beta_1^I \text{ INTERNAL}_i \\ & + \beta_1^M \text{ MENTAL}_i + \beta_1^O \text{ OTHER}_i + \phi_1 \text{POST}_i \\ & + \theta_1^S \text{ MUSCULOSKELETAL}_i \times \text{POST}_i + \theta_1^I \text{ INTERNAL}_i \times \text{POST}_i \\ & + \theta_1^M \text{ MENTAL}_i \times \text{POST}_i + \theta_1^O \text{ OTHER}_i \times \text{POST}_i + \epsilon_{1i} \end{aligned}$

(2.6) $\begin{aligned} \text{EMP}_i = {} & \alpha_2 + \gamma_2'X_{2i} + \beta_2^S \text{ MUSCULOSKELETAL}_i + \beta_2^I \text{ INTERNAL}_i \\ & + \beta_2^M \text{ MENTAL}_i + \beta_2^O \text{ OTHER}_i + \phi_2 \text{POST}_i \\ & + \theta_2^S \text{ MUSCULOSKELETAL}_i \times \text{POST}_i + \theta_2^I \text{ INTERNAL}_i \times \text{POST}_i \\ & + \theta_2^M \text{ MENTAL}_i \times \text{POST}_i + \theta_2^O \text{ OTHER}_i \times \text{POST}_i + \epsilon_{2i} \end{aligned}$

where LFP_i is equal to 1 if person i is in the labor force, 0 otherwise,
EMP_i is equal to 1 if person i is employed, 0 otherwise,
X_i is a set of covariates for each person (individual demographic characteristics),
MUSCULOSKELETAL_i is equal to 1 if person i has a musculoskeletal disability,[21]
INTERNAL_i is equal to 1 if person i has a disability involving the internal systems,
MENTAL_i is equal to 1 if person i has a mental disability,
OTHER_i is equal to 1 if person i has a disability classified as "other," and
POST_i is equal to 1 if person i is observed in 1992 or later.

Again, these equations are estimated via maximum likelihood as a bivariate probit with selection, where EMP_i is only observed if $\text{LFP}_i = 1$. In this framework, the type of disability is controlled for by dummy variables indicating whether the individual has a musculoskeletal, internal systems, mental, or other disability; and the time period is controlled for by a dummy variable indicating whether the ADA had been implemented yet or not. The coefficients of particular interest (θ_1^i and

$\theta_2^j, j = S,I,M,O$), therefore, allow us to calculate the labor force participation and employment changes among disabled workers post- versus
pre-ADA relative to the changes for nondisabled workers. Table 2.4
provides selected estimated coefficients and regression details.

The estimation results presented in Table 2.4 from the SIPP data
set are also consistent with the conclusions drawn using the CPS data:
labor force participation declined more for all classifications of disability, relative to nondisability, post- versus pre-ADA. However, employ-

**Table 2.4 Labor Force Participation and Employment Bivariate Probit
with Selection Results by Type of Disability, SIPP Combined
Years, 1986–1997**

Regressor	Labor force participation equation	Employment equation
MUSCULOSKELETAL = 1	−0.8253***	−0.2798***
	(0.0150)	(0.0281)
INTERNAL = 1	−0.9597***	−0.1660***
	(0.0192)	(0.0409)
MENTAL = 1	−1.2722***	−0.1599***
	(0.0237)	(0.0487)
OTHER = 1	−0.8396***	−0.3429***
	(0.0280)	(0.0508)
POST (year = 1992 or later) = 1	0.0305***	−0.0348***
	(0.0048)	(0.0077)
MUSCULOSKELETAL × POST = 1	−0.1416***	0.0542
	(0.0187)	(0.0348)
INTERNAL × POST = 1	−0.1137***	0.1693
	(0.0247)	(0.0532)
MENTAL × POST = 1	−0.0850***	0.1187**
	(0.0282)	(0.0573)
OTHER × POST = 1	−0.0829**	0.1484**
	(0.0360)	(0.0675)
Rho	−0.4799***	
	(0.0205)	
Log-likelihood	−292,164	
Number of observations	500,560	

NOTE: See notes to Table 2.3 regarding additional regressors. Standard errors are in
  parentheses.
*** = significant at the 99 percent confidence level.
** = significant at the 95 percent confidence level.

ment probabilities (controlling for labor force participation) *increased* significantly more for the disability classifications of MENTAL and OTHER than for the nondisabled, post- versus pre-ADA. Relative employment probabilities did not change significantly for those with musculoskeletal or internal disabilities.

While it is difficult to interpret the employment impact for those with disabilities classified as OTHER, the major role that those with mental disorders play in explaining the overall relative employment improvement is not surprising, given the attention paid to and policies developed for those with mental disabilities in recent years.[22] In addition, if we expect costs of accommodation to influence employment outcomes of the disabled, these results might suggest that accommodating workers with mental disabilities (such as through flexible work scheduling) has been relatively less expensive for employers than accommodating workers with musculoskeletal or internal disabilities (for example, through physical modification of the work environment).

EMPLOYMENT PROBABILITY AND FIRM SIZE

The phased-in nature of the ADA yields an additional dimension across which to examine its impact on employment.[23] After enactment in 1990, the ADA covered employers with 25 or more employees starting in 1992, and employers with 15 or more employees starting in 1994. One might expect a differential employment impact of the ADA based on whether a particular firm is covered by the legislation. In addition, because of the potential costs of accommodating workers' disabilities, there is reason to expect that disabled workers might migrate toward covered employers (based on size), toward employers who are more able to absorb the cost of accommodation (larger firms may have more resources to devote to such investments), and toward employers who can spread the fixed costs of accommodation across more workers (again, this would be true of larger firms). While most estimates indicate that per-worker costs of accommodations only range between $100 and $1,000, this expenditure is clearly easier to absorb for larger, more affluent firms (LaPlante 1992; Kujala 1996).[24] The federal government recognizes this burden to small business by making a targeted tax credit available for up to half of an accommodation expenditure that exceeds $250 but is less than $10,250 (Dykxhoorn and Sinning 1993; Hays 1999).

Figure 2.4 plots the distributions of disabled and nondisabled workers across firm sizes. Here, a small firm is one that employs fewer than 25 workers, a medium firm employs at least 25 but fewer than 100, and a large firm employs at least 100 workers.[25] The CPS began asking about the size (number of employees) of a worker's firm in 1988. This question refers to a person's main job during the previous year and is therefore available for the years 1987–1999. Large firms employ by far the greatest percentage of both disabled and nondisabled workers. While the average (over time) percentage in medium-sized firms is practically identical across disability status (14 percent), a greater proportion of nondisabled workers (62 percent versus 58 percent) is employed in large firms, and a greater proportion of disabled workers (28 percent versus 24 percent) is employed in small firms. As far as trends are concerned, nothing obvious is apparent from Figure 2.4. Trend regression indicates that there have been statistically significant declines in medium-firm employment among both disabled and nondisabled workers. While most of this decline among the nondisabled shifted toward small firms, the shift among the disabled was toward large firms. The analysis that follows will allow quantification of these movements and a direct comparison across disability status.

A multinomial logit analysis was undertaken to determine how the relative employment of disabled and nondisabled workers in different-sized firms has shifted over the entire time period for which firm size is available.[26] This approach allows us to specify multiple possible outcomes (e.g., employment in a small, medium, or large firm) as a function of a variety of observed characteristics and unobservable factors, recognizing that as one's probability of being in one firm size increases, the probability of being in another firm size necessarily decreases. A person's employment outcome is divided into three categories (where n refers to the number of employees at the worker's firm): 1) employed by a small ($n < 25$) firm, 2) employed by a medium ($25 \leq n < 100$) firm, and 3) employed by a large ($n \geq 100$) firm.[27]

It is assumed that the individual selects the firm size (*ceteris paribus*) that maximizes the utility gained from that choice. The employer plays a role in that decision by making different job packages available, such as wages and other characteristics. The probability of person i being employed in firm size 1 is defined as (where u refers to utility):

Figure 2.4 Distribution of Disabled and Nondisabled Workers across Firm Size, CPS, 1987–1999

(A) Disabled workers

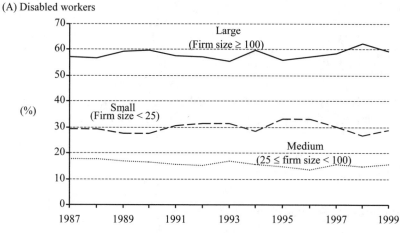

(B) Nondisabled workers

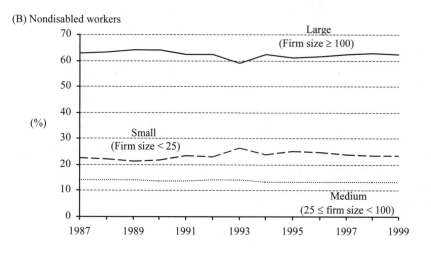

(2.7) $P_1 = P(n_i = 1) = P(u_{i1} > u_{ij})$ for $j = 2,3.$

Let

(2.8) $\dfrac{P_j}{P_j + P_3} = F(\beta_j'X)$ for $j = 1,2,$

where $F(\cdot)$ is the cumulative distribution function, X are individual characteristics, and β are parameter coefficients. This means that

(2.9) $\dfrac{P_j}{P_3} = \dfrac{F(\beta_j'X)}{1 - F(\beta_j'X)} = G(\beta_j'X)$ for $j = 1,2.$

Because of the rules of summation,

(2.10) $P_3 = 1 \Big/ \left[1 + \displaystyle\sum_{j=1}^{2} G(\beta_j'X) \right]$ and $P_j = \dfrac{G(\beta_j'X)}{1 + \displaystyle\sum_{j=1}^{2} G(\beta_j'X)}.$

If we let

(2.11) $G(\beta_j'X) = \exp(\beta_j'X)$ and Y_{ij}

$= \begin{cases} 1 \text{ if person } i \text{ falls in firm size category } j \\ 0 \text{ otherwise} \end{cases}$

the log likelihood function (ln L) can be written as

(2.12) $\ln L = \displaystyle\sum_{i=1}^{3} \sum_{j=1}^{3} Y_{ij} \ln P_{ij},$

where $P_{ij} = \dfrac{\exp(X_i'\beta_j)}{1 + \displaystyle\sum_{k=1}^{2} \exp(X_i'\beta_k)}$ and $P_{i3} = \dfrac{1}{1 + \displaystyle\sum_{k=1}^{2} \exp(X_i'\beta_k)}.$

The multinomial logit results in three sets of parameter estimates, each set describing the probability of one of the firm size outcomes.

Every person has a probability of being employed by each size firm, and those three probabilities sum to one (since the analysis is restricted to employed individuals). Figure 2.5 summarizes the predicted probabilities of disabled workers, relative to the predicted probabilities of nondisabled workers, being employed by each size firm for the years from 1987 to 1999.[28]

The probability of employment of disabled workers relative to nondisabled workers in both small- and medium-size firms declined over this time period, whereas the relative probability of employment of disabled workers in large firms increased.[29] This means that relative to nondisabled workers, disabled workers were increasingly likely to be employed in large firms between 1987 and 1999. This result is consistent with Kaye (2002), who finds growing employment rates among the disabled in "big-business" industries (500 or more employees). The increased probability of employment among larger firms may suggest that they have been able to accommodate (i.e., afford, spread costs over greater numbers of workers, find appropriate job matches) workers' disabilities more than small- or even medium-sized firms, and that disabled workers have found it fruitful to seek out jobs at the largest firms. In fact, large companies have typically been at the forefront of implementing costly accommodations, either because of public relations initiatives or because of other considerations not faced by smaller

Figure 2.5 Ratio of Predicted Employment Probabilities for Disabled versus Nondisabled Workers by Firm Size, CPS, 1987–1999

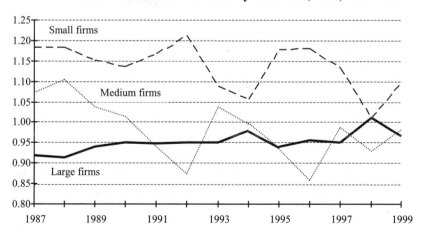

businesses (Johnson 1997). These visible efforts make larger companies more attractive for disabled job seekers. In addition, one study
has found that large firms are significantly more likely to comply with
the ADA and to have specific policies in place guiding the hiring of
workers with disabilities (Scheid 1998). It is important to point out,
however, that since the ADA has no affirmative action component, the
relative shift in employment of disabled workers toward larger firms is
not likely the result of active recruitment efforts.

Since employers with 25 or more workers were covered by the
ADA beginning in 1992, one additional computation can help to quantify any adjustment that may have occurred at that time in the relative
employment probabilities. Table 2.5 presents a form of differences-in-
differences-in-differences (DDD) calculation for the average predicted
probabilities of employment across firm size, time, and disability
status. These DDD results are not derived from an estimation procedure, but are merely the differences in predicted probabilities across
coverage, firm size, and time. The predicted probabilities from the

**Table 2.5 DDD Calculation for Average Predicted Probability of
Employment by Firm Size, Disability Status, and across Time,
CPS, 1987–1999**

Firm size / year	1987–91		1992–98	Time difference for a given firm size
A. Disabled workers				
$n \geq 25$	0.7434		0.7280	−0.0154
$n < 25$	0.2566		0.2720	0.0154
Firm size difference at a point in time	0.4868		0.4560	
Differences-in-differences		−0.0308		
B. Nondisabled workers				
$n \geq 25$	0.7798		0.7571	−0.0227
$n < 25$	0.2202		0.2429	0.0227
Firm size difference at a point in time	0.5596		0.5142	
Differences-in-differences		−0.0454		
DDD:		**0.0146**		

NOTE: n refers to the number of employees in the firm. Predicted probabilities for
each firm size from the multinomial logit results presented in Figure 2.3 are averaged
across the years indicated and disability status to obtain the average predicted probabilities.

multinomial logit estimation are used for differencing, and the probabilities for the medium and large firm sizes are combined to correspond to the coverage of the ADA beginning in 1992. This analysis is not as precise as we might like, since employers with 15 or more workers were covered by the ADA beginning in 1994, and since there are no standard errors available to determine significance of the results. Consequently, the results in Table 2.5 should be viewed only as suggestive. The DDD analysis suggests that covered disabled workers have, at most, a 1.5 percentage point greater probability of being employed, relative to noncovered disabled workers, post-ADA, relative to pre-ADA, relative to the employment probability differences among nondisabled workers.

CONCLUSIONS

The purpose of this chapter was to evaluate the relative employment experiences of disabled and nondisabled workers. A pooled, cross-sectional analysis determined that the joint labor force and employment probability of the disabled decreased significantly after implementation of the ADA relative to a nondisabled person's employment probability. This joint probability is influenced by both supply and demand factors and therefore confounds the employment experience of disabled workers with labor supply influences. In order to get a picture of the expected employment outcome, the unconditional employment probability was calculated. It was found that the unconditional employment probability among the disabled did not change after implementation of the ADA relative to the employment probability among the nondisabled. In other words, although improvements in relative employment outcomes have not been realized, there has not been the deterioration of the employment position of the disabled as claimed by others. This suggests that adjustments in the labor supply of disabled workers are not likely the result of feedback effects or fear of negative outcomes, since the employment outcomes for disabled workers relative to those of nondisabled workers did not deteriorate post-ADA. It was also shown that the decline in labor force participation was likely the result of the reclassification of nondisabled, nonparticipants as disabled, post-welfare reform and potentially in response to the growing generosity of disability benefit policies.

Analysis of the SIPP data produced a confirmation of the CPS results and allowed a closer evaluation of employment probabilities by type of disability. In fact, the SIPP results suggest that the relative employment position actually *improved*, with greater unconditional employment probabilities among the disabled post-ADA, compared to the nondisabled. It was found that those with mental disorders and those with disabilities classified as OTHER experienced the greatest positive employment impact of the ADA. Workers with musculoskeletal and internal system disabilities did not experience any different employment probability growth from those without disabilities.

Evidence that the cost of accommodation is not irrelevant in the labor market's adjustment to the ADA was found in a DDD analysis, which accounted for the size of a worker's employer, allowing for identification of disabled workers who were covered by the legislation and those who were not. Disabled workers employed by large or medium firms (covered employers) have, at most, a 1.5 percentage point greater probability of being employed, relative to disabled workers in small firms, post-ADA, relative to pre-ADA, relative to nondisabled workers. In addition, employment of disabled workers was shown to shift more towards large firms post-ADA than did employment of nondisabled workers. Since the fixed cost of disability accommodations can be spread over a greater number of workers in large firms, this result suggests that larger firms were better poised and able to absorb the costs of accommodations dictated by the ADA and/or better able to match disabled workers' job skills with recruitment needs.

Notes

1. Also see DeLeire (1997, Section 3).
2. See Table C.2 in Appendix C for the percentages used to generate Figure 2.1.
3. See Stern (1996).
4. It has also been suggested that persons with disabilities entering the labor force after the ADA will have more severe disabilities than those employed prior to the ADA, making the potential for "binding" accommodation requirements that much more likely and expensive (Chirikos 1991).
5. This model specification is similar to that familiar to most labor economists: controlling for selection into the labor market (or employment) when estimating a

wage equation. In that problem, we are interested in the (unconditional) expected wage for anyone in the population. By controlling for selection into the labor market (since we can only estimate the wage equation on those for whom we observe wages), we are able to make unconditional predictions that correspond to the population. If selection is not controlled for, the only prediction of wages that can be made is that conditional on labor force participation.

6. The bivariate probit model with selection gives rise to the following likelihood function:

$$\ln L = \sum_{\text{LFP}=1,\,\text{EMP}=1} \ln \Phi_2[\gamma_1' X_{1i}, \gamma_2' X_{2i}, \rho] +$$
$$\sum_{\text{LFP}=1,\text{EMP}=0} \ln \Phi_2[\gamma_1' X_{1i}, -\gamma_2' X_{2i}, \rho] + \sum_{\text{LFP}=0} \ln \Phi[-\gamma_1' X_{1i}),$$

where Φ_2 is the bivariate normal cumulative distribution function and Φ is the univariate normal cumulative distribution function.

7. This method of calculating the marginal effect of a change in a dummy variable is referred to as a measure of discrete change and is described in greater detail by Long (1997, pp. 135–138). Specifically, the average marginal impact of having a disability on the joint labor force and employment outcome is calculated as

$$\frac{1}{N}\sum_{i=1}^{N}\{P_i[\text{LFP}=1,\,\text{EMP}=1|X_i,\,\text{DISABLE}=1] - P_i[\text{LFP}=1,\,\text{EMP}=1|X_i,\,\text{DISABLE}=0]\},$$

and the average marginal impact of having a disability on the unconditional probability of employment is calculated as

$$\frac{1}{N}\sum_{i=1}^{N}\{P_i[\text{EMP}=1|X_i,\,\text{DISABLE}=1] - P_i[\text{EMP}=1|X_i,\,\text{DISABLE}=0]\}.$$ Both of

these are calculated, of course, using the parameter estimates obtained from the bivariate probit model with selection detailed in endnote 6.

8. This model specification allows a comparison to results with earlier studies, as well (through calculation of the joint probability).

9. See Table C.3 in Appendix C for the numbers used to generate Figure 2.2 (numbers in column 3 minus numbers in column 1).

10. In addition, Stern (1996) presents empirical evidence that labor supply decisions of disabled people are driven more by labor supply factors than by labor demand factors. Also see Averett, et al. (1999) for further evidence on this point.

11. One can easily show that, for C > 0 for $\text{LFPR}_d = C/(C + D)$, $\partial \text{LFPR}_d/\partial D < 0$ and $\partial \text{LFPR}_d/\partial C > 0$.

12. Acemoglu and Angrist (2001) dismiss this theory by showing that controlling for receipt of disability benefits only marginally impacts their results. They fail to point out, however, that the receipt of benefits will reflect only a fraction of the desire to receive benefits (see Kubik 1999). Consequently, the actual impact of increasing program generosity on the disability status change for nonparticipants could be much larger than that measured by growing recipiency.

13. These trend coefficient estimates for each cell were obtained from simple linear regressions of the percentage of people represented in that cell as a function of a time trend corresponding to the period 1990–2000, in order to focus on post-ADA changes.

14. The strategy described here can be likened to the popular differences-in-differences (DD) methodology, but it is applied to a nonlinear statistical model.

15. Acemoglu and Angrist (2001, Appendix A) show that results are fairly consistent across a variety of sample restrictions based on differences between the 1993 and 1994 samples (crossing the survey modification time period). Consequently, it is not expected that the results reported here are significantly biased by changes in the CPS survey design.

16. The cyclicality of disabled and nondisabled employment is explored by Burkhauser, Daly, and Houtenville (2000), although, like Acemoglu and Angrist (2001) and DeLeire (2000), their analysis confounds employment outcomes with labor supply effects.

17. See endnote 7.

18. The remaining parameter estimates are consistent with labor/leisure choice theory. For example, higher nonlabor income and being female lead to lower labor force participation, and the age/participation profile is concave. They also conform to standard human capital theory with more education and greater labor market experience (measured through number of weeks worked last year) leading to a greater probability of employment.

19. The marginal effect on the joint probability outcome was -3 percentage points (column 3, last row). While not directly comparable, DeLeire (2000) estimates a 7.2 percentage point drop in employment among all disabled men, and Acemoglu and Angrist (2001) estimate a 10–15 percentage point drop in the number of weeks worked by the disabled. Again, these results are analogous to the joint probability calculated here, although not surprisingly of slightly varying magnitude given the differences in data used (DeLeire) and in estimation procedure and model specification (DeLeire and Acemoglu and Angrist).

20. See Appendix B for the source of classification of disability.

21. The musculoskeletal grouping includes disabilities involving the special senses (e.g., hearing, sight).

22. The President's Committee on Employment of People with Disabilities had placed an emphasis in the late 1990s on individuals with mental impairments. This committee has more recently been replaced by the Presidential Task Force on Employment of Adults with Disabilities. Information about the activities of this task force can be found on the U.S. Department of Labor web site, <http://www.dol.gov/_sec/programs/ptfead/>.

23. Chay (1996) and Carrington, McCue, and Pierce (2000) represent other research exploiting the natural phase-in periods across firm size or geographic differences in dates of implementation in order to measure the labor market impact of social policy legislation.

24. In addition to the direct costs of accommodation, efficiency costs not directly absorbed by the employer, but felt by the labor market as a whole, are identified by Rosen (1991).

25. This definition of small, medium, and large firms follows that of Acemoglu and Angrist (2001); the definition will change in the next chapter.

26. Multinomial logits have come under frequent criticism because of the assumption of independence of irrelevant alternatives (IIA) that is implied by the logit specification. Alternative specifications that retain the desired probability structure (i.e., multinomial probit) are riddled with their own problems and not considered here to add value greater than the cost imposed. It has been pointed out that under the framework of what is called a "universal" logit, the estimation procedure can be applied, but the utility interpretation of the structural estimates is lost. In addition, the more regressors included to describe the multiple outcomes, the less bothersome is the assumption of IIA. For these reasons, the logit structure is retained. For further discussion on these points, see Ben-Akiva and Lerman (1985, section 5.2) and Moffitt (1999, pp. 1382–1387).

27. The results of this analysis are relevant for *workers* only and not generalizable to the entire population.

28. The predicted probabilities are found in Table C.4 in Appendix C.

29. A firm-size analysis was also undertaken by Acemoglu and Angrist (2001). Since they did not restrict their analysis to workers, they found that relative employment declined across all firm sizes (compared with not working), and that there was no change in relative employment of disabled workers in large firms, as compared with the nondisabled.

3
Compensation: Wages and Benefits

The issue of compensation has generated numerous contributions to the demand side of the disability literature. For example, Haveman and Wolfe (1990) evaluate the economic well-being (in which a major factor is earnings, or compensation) of the disabled over an extended period of time (1962–1984). A large part of their measure of well-being, however, is accounted for by transfer income (a nonlabor market source of income).[1] In addition, while Salkever and Domino (1997), Johnson and Lambrinos (1985), and Baldwin and Johnson (2000) have examined the issue of wage discrimination against the disabled, evidence on how these measures of discrimination have changed over time is sparse (see DeLeire 2001).

Depending on the nature of the impairment, one would expect a disabled worker to be less productive than an otherwise identical nondisabled worker; thus, lower wages would be seen for disabled workers. The implementation of a policy that is expected to raise productivity, however, would increase those individuals' wages. The ADA, through its accommodation requirements, should unambiguously increase the productivity of disabled workers. The impact of this process on workers' earnings, however, is uncertain. If productivity is increased by more than the cost of accommodations, wages of disabled workers should rise. If, on the other hand, the cost of accommodation exceeds the gains in productivity, disabled workers are likely to bear some of the increased costs through lower wages. In addition, since accommodation should not impact the productivity of workers not in need of those accommodations (i.e., nondisabled workers), we should not observe a substantial wage change for nondisabled workers post-ADA.

The CPS contains data on wages paid and hours employed for all workers. Information on the availability of health insurance and pension plans through one's employer is also available. This chapter compares how relative earnings for workers with disabilities have changed over time and if there was any significant alteration coinciding with the implementation of the ADA. These comparisons are also made across types of disability with the help of the SIPP data set. Earnings of disabled workers are compared with those of workers without disabilities to determine whether there has been any improvement in the compensation disparity over time and how much of that disparity is left unexplained by differences in productivity (i.e., potential discrimination), particularly around the period that the ADA became law and was fully implemented. The methodology employed will also allow an examination of how much of the earnings disparity is accounted for by different representations of disabled workers across occupations and/or industries. Nonwage compensation is growing in importance for all employees and may be of particular importance to disabled workers. As such, the probability of being covered by health insurance and a pension plan is evaluated as a function of disability status, also across time. These probabilities are compared, again, to see if any change occurred when the ADA was implemented.

WAGE LEVELS

Figure 3.1 depicts the average real (1982–1984 = 100) hourly wages for disabled and non-disabled workers for each year from 1981

Figure 3.1 Average Real Hourly Wages, CPS, 1981–2000

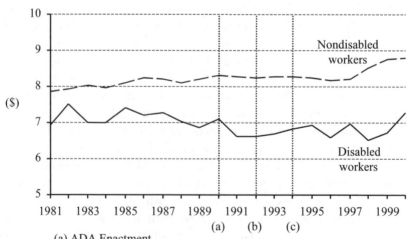

(a) ADA Enactment
(b) ADA Phase I
(c) ADA Phase II

to 2000. As theorized, wages for disabled workers lie below those of nondisabled workers for every year, although these raw figures do not control for differences in human capital or other demographic and job characteristics. Real wages of nondisabled workers exhibit a clear upward trend (a significant raw trend average of about 0.03 of a percentage point per year), and real wages of disabled workers exhibit a downward trend (a significant average of about −0.02 of a percentage point per year, in spite of the recent upward swing). The net result is a growing differential between wages of nondisabled and disabled workers. These relative trends will be examined to determine whether there was a significant difference pre- and post-ADA after controlling for individual and job characteristics. In addition, the wage differential will be decomposed to determine what factors are the greatest contributors to its level and its growth. For example, it could be the case that wages are falling among disabled workers because the nature of disabilities is becoming more severe in the population (Kaye 2002), making disabled workers as a whole less productive. Alternatively, the human capital of disabled workers may be deteriorating for some reason, disabled workers are shifting to lower-paying jobs, or employers may be passing along the costs of accommodations through lower wages for disabled workers.

Splitting the time series, the negative trend in wages for disabled workers observed in Figure 3.1 is clearly driven by the early years (a significant average decline of 1 percentage point per year from 1981 to 1991), while the years between 1992 and 2000 exhibit no trend at all, statistically. One could interpret this as a positive outcome of the ADA if the policy actually halted, or mitigated, a long-running downward trend in wages of disabled workers. However, this observation tells us nothing about the relative wage trend or components of the differential.

DIFFERENCES IN WAGES OVER TIME

Pooled, Cross-Sectional Analysis

The first analysis of wages in this chapter is a simple, pooled, cross-sectional one.[2] A linear relationship is specified in which the log of real wages is a function of demographic and job characteristics, as well as indicators for disability status, time period, and the interaction between disability status and time. The following specification is estimated via OLS for the time period 1984–2000:[3]

$$(3.1) \quad \text{LNRWAGE}_i = \alpha + \gamma'X_i + \beta_1\text{DISABLE}_i + \beta_2\text{POST}_i \\ + \beta_3\text{DISABLE}_i \times \text{POST}_i + \epsilon_i$$

where LNRWAGE$_i$ is the natural log hourly real (1982–1984 = 100) wage of worker i,

X_i is a set of covariates for each person (demographic and job characteristics),

DISABLE$_i$ is equal to 1 if person i has a work-limiting disability, and

POST$_i$ is equal to one if person i is observed in 1992 or later.

The affected group (the disabled) is controlled for by a dummy variable indicating whether the individual has a work-limiting disability, and the time period is controlled for by a dummy variable indicating whether the ADA had been implemented yet or not. The coefficient of interest (β_3) measures the change in real wages of disabled workers, relative to nondisabled workers, after implementation of the ADA, relative to before implementation. In other words, β_3 tells us how wages changed for disabled workers versus nondisabled workers. X_i includes individual demographic and job characteristics detailed in Table 3.1, which contains the estimation results; γ are additional parameter coefficients to be estimated, and ϵ_i is the random error term.

Since wages are observed for workers only, and since the characteristics of workers may be changing over time in unobservable ways, it is important to control for any potential unobserved self-selection into the labor market. Consequently, Equation 3.1 is modified by simply adding the standard inverse-Mills ratio obtained from a first-stage probit estimation of a labor force participation/employment equation. This standard Heckman (1979) two-step procedure for controlling for self-selection is presented in greater detail in the section on wage decompositions. Briefly, including the selection term in the regression allows β_3 to be interpreted as relevant for the entire disabled and nondisabled population, even though the sample for the regression included workers only. The parameters of the model are identified

Table 3.1 OLS Selectivity-Corrected Regression Results for Log Real Wages, across Disability Status and ADA Implementation, CPS, 1984–2000

Regressor	Parameter estimates
Intercept	1.1277***
	(0.0121)
Age	0.0498***
	(0.0059)
Age squared	−0.0005
	(0.0023)
Female = 1	−0.2249***
	(0.0016)
Nonwhite = 1	−0.0434***
	(0.0018)
Single household = 1	−0.0524***
	(0.0015)
High school grad = 1	0.0834***
	(0.0020)
Some college = 1	0.1614***
	(0.0022)
College grad = 1	0.2806***
	(0.0025)
Advanced degree = 1	0.3072***
	(0.0013)
Hours	0.0024
	(0.0055)
Union = 1	0.1976***
	(0.0005)
DISABLE = 1	−0.1719***
	(0.0018)
POST (year = 1992 or later) = 1	−0.0033***
	(0.0011)
DISABLE × POST = 1	−0.0286***
	(0.0064)
$\hat{\lambda}$ (selection term)	0.0327***
	(0.0043)
Number of observations	766,060
F statistic	18,486***
Adjusted R^2	0.4279

NOTE: Other regressors included in the estimation, but not reported here, include seven industry and five occupation dummy variables, region, and government employer dummy variables.
*** = significant at the 99 percent confidence level. Asymptotically consistent standard errors are in parentheses.

through inclusion of some regressors in the first-stage probit estimation that are not in the wage regression; these regressors include nonlabor income and an indicator of whether the person worked last year or not. Since the purpose of this two-stage estimation approach is merely to obtain unbiased estimates of the coefficients in the wage equation, interpretation of those coefficients is not changed by controlling for selection.

All of the parameter estimates in Table 3.1 are of the magnitude and direction one might expect from standard human capital and other labor market theories. For example, women and nonwhites earn lower wages, union workers earn higher wages, and increased wages accrue to those with greater levels of education. The positive coefficient on the selection term $(\hat{\lambda})$ indicates positive selection into the labor market; the more likely someone is to enter the labor market, the more likely he or she will earn a wage above the population average.

The coefficient on the interaction term DISABLE × POST is -0.0286 (and significantly different from zero), indicating that disabled workers experienced about a 3 percent decline in wages, relative to nondisabled workers, post-ADA implementation, relative to pre-implementation. In other words, wages of the disabled fell by 3 percent more post-ADA than the wages of the nondisabled. This finding is not consistent with the result of DeLeire (2000), who found no significant change in the wages of disabled workers relative to those of nondisabled workers, post-ADA.[4] However, the result does suggest that the cost of accommodating disabled workers, overall, potentially exceeded their gains in productivity.[5] It is important to note that this result was obtained by controlling for job characteristic differences, such as hours of work, occupation, and industry. The potential implication of shifts in occupation and industry distributions on these results is explored in Chapter 4.

Evidence from the SIPP

The pooled, cross-sectional analysis specified in Equation 3.1 was reestimated using the SIPP data set for the years 1986–1997 (and, again, controlling for selection of workers into the labor market through a two-step estimation strategy). Selected coefficient estimates from the reestimation are presented in Table 3.2. While not statistically

Table 3.2 OLS Selectivity-Corrected DD Regression Results for Log Real Wages, across Disability Status and Type of Disability Status, SIPP 1986–1997

Regressor	Parameter estimates	
	Disability indicator only	Type of disability indicated
DISABLE = 1	−0.1535***	—
	(0.0027)	
POST (year = 1992 or later) = 1	−0.0515***	−0.0305***
	(0.0017)	(0.0017)
DISABLE × POST = 1	−0.0070	—
	(0.0072)	
MUSCULOSKELETAL = 1	—	−0.1230***
		(0.0084)
INTERNAL = 1	—	−0.1537***
		(0.0115)
MENTAL = 1	—	−0.3427***
		(0.0157)
OTHER = 1	—	−0.1124***
		(0.0153)
MUSCULOSKELETAL × POST = 1	—	−0.0424 ***
		(0.0098)
INTERNAL × POST = 1	—	0.0125
		(0.0148)
MENTAL × POST = 1	—	0.0220
		(0.0183)
OTHER × POST = 1	—	−0.0130
		(0.0193)
$\hat{\lambda}$ (selection term)	0.0046	0.0116*
	(0.0067)	(0.0065)
Number of observations	353,651	287,343
F statistic	8,855	6,502
Adjusted R^2	0.4289	0.4489

NOTE: Other regressors included in the estimation, but not reported here, include seven industry and five occupation dummy variables, hours of work, age, age squared, and race, education, union, gender, marital status, region, and government employer dummy variables. Asymptotically consistent standard errors are in parentheses.
*** = significant at the 99 percent confidence level.
* = significant at the 90 percent confidence level.

significant, the negative coefficient on the DISABLE × POST regressor is at least consistent (in sign) with the results obtained from the CPS data.

Table 3.2 presents an additional specification, which identifies type of disability. In the following equation, the impact of a worker's disability on the real wage is allowed to vary by type of impairment:[6]

$$(3.2) \quad \text{LNRWAGE}_i = \alpha + \gamma'X_i + \beta_1^S \text{ MUSCULOSKELETAL}_i + \beta_1^I \text{ INTERNAL}_i$$
$$+ \beta_1^M \text{ MENTAL}_i + \beta_1^O \text{ OTHER}_i + \beta_2 \text{POST}_i$$
$$+ \beta_3^S \text{ MUSCULOSKELETAL}_i \times \text{POST}_i + \beta_3^I \text{ INTERNAL}_i$$
$$\times \text{POST}_i + \beta_3^M \text{ MENTAL}_i \times \text{POST}_i$$
$$+ \beta_3^O \text{ OTHER} \times \text{POST}_i + \epsilon_i$$

where LNRWAGE$_i$ is the natural log hourly real (1982–1984 = 100) wage of worker i,

X_i is a set of covariates for each person (individual demographic characteristics),

MUSCULOSKELETAL$_i$ is equal to 1 if person i has a musculoskeletal disability,[7]

INTERNAL$_i$ is equal to 1 if person i has a disability involving the internal systems,

MENTAL$_i$ is equal to 1 if person i has a mental disability,

OTHER$_i$ is equal to 1 if person i has a disability classified as "other," and

POST$_i$ is equal to 1 if person i is observed in 1992 or later.

In this framework, the type of disability is controlled for by dummy variables indicating whether the individual has a musculoskeletal, internal systems, mental, or other limitation, and the time period is controlled for by a dummy variable indicating whether the ADA had been implemented yet or not. The coefficients of interest (β_3^j, $j = S,I,M,O$), therefore, measure the change in log real wages of workers with each type of disability, relative to nondisabled workers, after implementation of the ADA, relative to before implementation. X_i includes individual demographic and job characteristics, detailed in Table 3.2. Again, selection into the labor market has been controlled for.[8]

As it turns out, the type of disability that appears to be driving the observed overall decline in real wages of disabled workers relative to nondisabled workers, post-ADA, is musculoskeletal. The real wages of workers with musculoskeletal disabilities declined 4 percent more than for workers without disabilities post-ADA, relative to pre-ADA (the coefficient on MUSCULOSKELETAL × POST is −0.0424). This is of interest because it lends support to the theory that wages of disabled workers are sensitive to the degree of accommodation required of the employer. Whereas accommodation of a worker with a mental disorder, such as depression, may simply be a flexible work schedule, individuals with musculoskeletal disabilities might require more investment in infrastructure, such as specially constructed office furniture.[9] In light of evidence that the typical per-worker cost of accommodation is fairly modest (on the order of $100–$1,000), according to Kujala (1996), employers may be setting wages on some perceived higher cost.

Firm Size Analysis

The CPS contains a question about how large (i.e., number of employees) a worker's main employer was in the previous year. Given that the ADA covers employers only of certain size, this information can be exploited to perform an additional analysis across covered and noncovered disabled workers. Covered disabled workers would be those employed by a firm with 25 or more employees in 1992 or later or employed by a firm with 15 or more employees in 1994 or later. Unfortunately, classifications of firms with fewer than 25 employees were not made until the 1992 survey year, which limits the amount of pre-ADA data available for the analysis. The post-ADA years were restricted to balance this survey-imposed limitation. The following model will be estimated twice: once for a large versus not-large firm classification, and a second time for a medium versus small firm classification. Selection into the labor market will be controlled for in both estimations, using the standard Heckman (1979) two-step procedure detailed later in this chapter. The impact on wages across firm size (ADA coverage) is obtained from the following linear specification:

$$
\begin{aligned}
\textbf{(3.3)} \quad \text{LNRWAGE}_i = {} & \alpha + \gamma' X_i + \beta_1 \text{DISABLE}_i + \beta_2 \text{POST}_i + \beta_3 \text{COVERED}_i \\
& + \beta_4 \text{DISABLE}_i \times \text{POST}_i + \beta_5 \text{DISABLE}_i \times \text{COVERED}_i \\
& + \beta_6 \text{POST}_i \times \text{COVERED}_i \\
& + \beta_7 \text{DISABLE}_i \times \text{POST}_i \times \text{COVERED}_i + \epsilon_i
\end{aligned}
$$

where LNRWAGE$_i$ is the natural log hourly real (1982–1984 = 100)
    wage of worker i,
    X_i is a set of covariates for each person (demographic and job
    characteristics),
    DISABLE$_i$ is equal to 1 if person i has a work-limiting disability,
    POST$_i$ is equal to 1 if person i is observed in 1992–1993 for the
    large firm analysis and equal to 1 if person i is observed in
    1994–1996 for the medium firm analysis,[10] and
    COVERED$_i$ is equal to 1 if person i is employed by a firm covered
    by ADA legislation.

The dummy variables (DISABLE, POST, and COVERED) control for the
time-invariant characteristics of the affected group, disabled workers
(β_1); the time-series changes in wages (β_2); and the time-invariant characteristics of the covered firm size, large or medium (β_3). The second-
level interactions control for changes over time for disabled workers
(β_4), time-invariant characteristics of disabled workers in the covered
firm size (β_5), and changes over time within a covered firm size (β_6).
The third-level interaction (β_7) captures all variation in wages specific
to the disabled workers (relative to nondisabled workers) in the covered
firm size (relative to uncovered firms) in the years after the firm was
covered by ADA (relative to before ADA). The uncovered firms for
the large firm analysis contain both small- and medium-sized organizations ($n < 25$). Uncovered firms for the medium firm analysis contain
small entities only ($n < 10$); large firms are not included in the medium
firm analysis.[11] The results of the medium firm analysis are somewhat
contaminated by the fact that the ADA covers firms with 15 or more
employees, so the indicator for medium firms contains some employers
not technically covered by the ADA (those who employ more than 10
but fewer than 15 workers). The covariates included in the regression
are detailed in Table 3.3, which presents the estimation results.

The results in Table 3.3 indicate the following. Workers in large
and medium (covered) firms earn higher wages than workers in small
firms (see the coefficient on COVERED); disabled workers in large and
medium firms earn higher wages, holding everything else constant,
than nondisabled workers in those firms (see the coefficient on DISABLE
× COVERED); and wages of disabled workers covered by the ADA did
not change post-ADA relative to disabled workers not covered (see the

Table 3.3 OLS Selectivity-Corrected Regression Results for Log Real Wages, across Disability Status, Covered Firm Size, and ADA Implementation, CPS

Regressor	Large firms (n≥25) as covered group	Medium firms (10≤n<25) as covered group
Intercept	4.4252***	3.9121***
	(0.0368)	(0.0820)
Age	0.0838***	0.0966***
	(0.0169)	(0.0266)
Age squared	−0.0009	−0.0011
	(0.0061)	(0.0131)
Female = 1	−0.3505***	−0.4264***
	(0.0237)	(0.0357)
Nonwhite = 1	−0.0079*	0.0041
	(0.0044)	(0.0098)
Single household = 1	−0.0905***	−0.0683***
	(0.0013)	(0.0023)
High school grad = 1	0.1374***	0.2670***
	(0.0032)	(0.0099)
Some college = 1	0.2023***	0.3086***
	(0.0055)	(0.0112)
College grad = 1	0.3093***	0.3965***
	(0.0055)	(0.0102)
Advanced degree = 1	0.4246***	0.5948***
	(0.0064)	(0.0124)
DISABLE = 1	−0.2780***	−0.4490***
	(0.0047)	(0.0210)
POST = 1	−0.0273***	0.1071**
	(0.0057)	(0.0081)
COVERED = 1	0.0982***	0.1174***
	(0.0047)	(0.0086)
DISABLE × POST = 1	−0.0570*	0.0317
	(0.0322)	(0.0431)
DISABLE × COVERED = 1	0.0572**	0.1074**
	(0.0264)	(0.0492)
POST × COVERED = 1	0.0245***	−0.0146
	(0.0066)	(0.0123)
DISABLE × POST × COVERED = 1	0.0517	−0.0879
	(0.0382)	(0.0707)

Table 3.3 (continued)

Regressor	Large firms (n≥25) as covered group	Medium firms (10≤n<25) as covered group
λ (selection term)	−0.2767***	0.0897
	(0.0279)	(0.0735)
Number of observations	182,318	55,459
F statistic	5,253	1,048
Adjusted R²	0.51	0.40

NOTE: Reference group for large firm analysis is small and medium firms (n<25); reference group for medium firm analysis is small firms only (n<10). Other regressors included in the estimation, but not reported here, include seven industry and five occupation dummy variables, and region, central city, benefit receipt, and government employer dummy variables. For the large firm comparison, POST = 0 for 1990–91 and POST = 1 for 1992–93. For the medium firm comparison, POST = 0 for 1991–93 and POST = 1 for 1994–96. Asymptotically consistent standard errors are in parentheses.
*** = significant at the 99 percent confidence level.
** = significant at the 95 percent confidence level.
* = significant at the 90 percent confidence level.

coefficient on DISABLE × POST × COVERED, which is not significant). The implication is that the decline in wages of disabled workers relative to those of nondisabled workers found in Tables 3.1 and 3.2 (and in Table 3.3 by the coefficient on DISABLE × POST) is attributable to something *other* than ADA coverage.

It is tempting to attribute the wage decline among disabled workers relative to nondisabled workers found earlier as indication that firms are passing accommodation costs on to disabled workers through lower pay. However, given that the wage difference between covered and noncovered disabled workers does not change post-ADA, there must be some other explanation than direct accommodation costs for the decline in wages relative to those of nondisabled workers. In other words, if the lower wages among disabled workers were the result of accommodation costs directly, then the wages of covered workers should fall relative to those of noncovered workers (whose employers are not required to incur the cost of accommodation). This is not what we see from the firm-size analysis. It appears that all disabled workers (covered or not) are suffering some ramifications of the ADA not directly attributable to the costs of accommodating their disabilities. The

ADA may have created an environment in which firms view all disabled workers as a hiring risk (perhaps through fear of litigation upon termination), and are passing that perceived greater risk on through lower wages.

WAGE DECOMPOSITION

This section decomposes the wage differentials observed in Figure 3.1 to determine which factors have the greatest influence over their levels and growth. Standard log wage equations are estimated separately for disabled and nondisabled workers. The following specification, presented for person i, is estimated separately for each year. In these equations, "nd" denotes nondisabled and "d" denotes disabled:

(3.4) $\ln W_{ind} = X_{ind}\beta_{nd} + \epsilon_{ind}$

$\ln W_{id} = X_{id}\beta_d + \epsilon_{id}$

where $\ln W_i$ is the natural log hourly wage of workers,

X_i are explanatory variables,

β are coefficients to be estimated, and

ϵ_i is the random error term.

As was seen in Chapter 2, there may exist significant self-selection into the labor market, particularly among the disabled population. In order to obtain an estimate of β representative of the population, this selection is controlled for using the standard Heckman (1979) two-step procedure.[12] The first stage of this procedure involves estimating a binary choice model of the following form:

(3.5) $\tilde{Y}_i = Z_i\gamma + u_i$, $\qquad u_i \sim N(0,1)$

where Z_i are explanatory variables, γ are parameters to be estimated, u_i is the normally distributed random error, and individual i enters the labor force if $\tilde{Y}_i > 0$. Since $\tilde{Y}_i$ is unobserved, a binary variable, Y_i, is defined as

(3.6) $Y_i = \begin{cases} 1 \\ 0 \end{cases}$ as $\tilde{Y}_i \overset{>}{\underset{\leq}{}} 0.$

The parameters, γ, are estimated via maximum likelihood probit, and the inverse-Mill's ratio is constructed for inclusion in the wage equations, which are then estimated via OLS. The modified wage equations are

(3.7) $\ln W_{ind} = X'_{ind} \beta_{nd} + \delta_{nd} \hat{\lambda}_{ind} + v_{ind},$
$\ln W_{id} = X'_{id} \beta_d + \delta_d \hat{\lambda}_{id} + v_{id},$

where all variables are as previously defined, $\hat{\lambda}_{ij} = \dfrac{\varphi(Z_{ij}\gamma_j)}{\Phi(Z_{ij}\gamma_j)}, j = $ d, nd, and v_i is the newly defined random error.

The parameter values that result from OLS estimation of the relationships in Equation 7 can be used to decompose the wage differential between disabled and nondisabled workers as follows:[13]

(3.8) $\overline{\ln W}_{nd} - \overline{\ln W}_d = \sum_k \hat{\beta}_{knd}(\overline{X}_{knd} - \overline{X}_{kd}) + \sum_k \overline{X}_{kd}(\hat{\beta}_{knd} - \hat{\beta}_d)$
$+ (\hat{\delta}_{nd}\overline{\lambda}_{nd} - \hat{\delta}_d\overline{\lambda}_d).$

The first term on the right-hand side reflects the role of differences in characteristics (endowments) that disabled and nondisabled workers bring to the labor market; it is referred to as the "endowment effect." The second term represents the differences among groups of workers in how their characteristics are valued in the workplace. This second term is often referred to as the "coefficient effect" or the "unexplained portion" and is cautiously attributed to discriminatory behavior on the part of the employer. The third term reflects the role of selection into the labor market (across disability status). The selectivity-corrected wage differential is calculated by subtracting the third (selectivity effect) term from the observed wage differential.

Figure 3.2 presents the results from this empirical analysis. The solid and dashed lines that move together toward the bottom of the figure represent the observed wage differential and the wage differen-

Figure 3.2 Observed and Selectivity-Corrected Wage Differentials and the Coefficient Effect as Percentage of Corrected Wage Differential, CPS, 1981–2000

tial corrected for selection, respectively. The dotted line represents the coefficient effect as a percentage of the corrected wage differential.[14]

Observed and Selectivity-Corrected Wage Differentials

Since 1981 (the earliest year of data), there is a clear and persistent increase in both the observed and selectivity-corrected wage differentials between disabled and nondisabled workers. Both differentials show that over this whole time period, nondisabled workers earned, on average, wages that were 23 percent higher than those of disabled workers. In addition, the corrected wage differential increased from 13 percent to 30 percent, indicating a deterioration of earnings of disabled workers relative to nondisabled workers over this time period. The decline in relative earnings is consistent with a downward trend identified by Haveman and Wolfe (1990) beginning in 1974. However, the growth in the wage differential appears to have been mitigated since 1992; the selectivity-corrected wage differential grew from 13 to 29 percent between 1981 and 1992, and has hovered around a mean of 28 percent since 1992, which was the first year of implementation of the ADA.

In addition, and particularly since 1996, individual selection into the labor market, or differences in selection between disabled and nondisabled workers, does not seem to be biasing the observed wage differentials between the two groups. The one exception to this might be the period 1992–1995. During this four-year span, the observed wage differential underrepresented the wage differential corrected for selection. The implication of this is that disabled workers were positively selecting into the labor market to a greater extent than nondisabled workers, driving the observed wage of disabled workers as a whole upward (and the wage differential downward). This is consistent with the labor force participation decline observed in Chapter 2, if the disabled labor force nonparticipants beginning around 1992 had systematically lower earnings potential than the disabled persons who stayed in the labor market. This would likely be the case as a result of the flow of Aid to Families with Dependent Children (AFDC) recipients to SSI (Lewin Group 1999). This result is not consistent, however, with the conjecture that the disabled workers entering the labor force post-ADA were those with the most limiting disabilities (Chirikos 1991). Whatever might have been making the observed and selectivity-corrected wage differentials diverge in the mid 1990s seems to have disappeared, since the two series have basically followed identical paths since 1996. The implication of this is that since 1996, selection into the labor market has had essentially the same impact on wages for disabled and nondisabled workers; self-selection explains none of the remaining wage differentials since that time.

Potential Wage Discrimination against Disabled Workers

The dotted line in the top part of Figure 3.2 reflects the coefficient effect as a percent of the corrected wage differential. Over the entire time period, the coefficient effect averages 77 percent of the corrected wage differential, or clearly a majority of the difference in wages between disabled and nondisabled workers. While there is quite a bit of variation over the years, the coefficient effect dominates the endowment effect in each year. The regressors in each year explain the usual 30–40 percent of the variation in wages of disabled workers and about 45 percent of the variation in wages of nondisabled workers (as indicated by the adjusted R^2 of the regressions). Consequently, interpreting the entire coefficient effect as an indication of discrimination would not be prudent. However, given the relative magnitude of the coefficient effect, the expected success in explaining wage variation, and the number of observable characteristics included in the regression, it is also unlikely that the coefficient effect can be completely dismissed as the result of unmeasured characteristics of either the disabled or nondisabled. Using data from the SIPP, Baldwin and Johnson (1995, 2000) also find that the coefficient effect is larger than the endowment effect as a percentage of the selectivity-corrected differential in 1984 and in 1990. Using a similar methodology and data from 1972, Johnson and Lambrinos (1985) show that only 34–40 percent of the wage differential between disabled and nondisabled workers was left unexplained by differences in endowments. Examining SIPP data from 1984 and 1993, DeLeire (2001) finds that only between 5 and 8 percent of the earnings gap is attributable to the coefficient effect.

Examining the endowment and coefficient effects in greater detail, it is of interest to see which set of regressors makes the largest contributions to these components. Table 3.4 presents the median contribution (across years) of the groups of regressors that control for occupation, industry, and education. While the contributions vary across the years, these median values represent the typical scenario (i.e., there is no obvious trend in any of these contributing factors), and it is usually the case that occupation and education were the largest

Table 3.4 Contribution of Regressors to Log Wage Differentials, Median across Years, CPS, 1981–2000

	Contribution to the endowment effect	Contribution to the coefficient effect
Occupation	0.0452	0.0424
Industry	0.0085	0.0817
Education	0.0363	−0.0419
Median total effects	0.0768	0.1738

NOTE: The contributions of occupation, industry, and education do not add up to the total effect because these numbers represent the median across all years and also do not represent all regressors in the wage regression.

contributors to the endowment effect and that industry was the largest contributor to the coefficient effect. It is also of interest to note that in 18 of the 20 years, the return to education acted to *decrease* the wage differential between disabled and nondisabled workers (the contribution of the education regressors to the coefficient effect was negative). In other words, disabled workers typically received a greater return to their educational investment than nondisabled workers.[15] Regarding endowments, it is clear that nondisabled workers bring greater educational attainment to the labor market and are more likely to locate in the higher-paying occupations and industries (a phenomenon that will be explored more fully in Chapter 4); these observations are evidenced by positive contributions made by the occupation, industry, and education regressors to the endowment effect.

An additional feature provided by the analysis is that the relative importance of the coefficient effect over time can be evaluated. While perhaps not very obvious in Figure 3.2, there is actually a (slightly) significant negative trend in the coefficient effect as a percentage of the corrected wage differential. On average, the contribution of the coefficient effect to the overall wage differential declines an average of 1.7 percentage points per year from 1981 to 2000.[16] In addition, the endowment effect as a percentage of the corrected wage differential increased an average of 0.6 of a percentage point per year over the same time period.[17] Consequently, another silver lining to the rising wage differential between disabled and nondisabled workers, and to the large portion of that differential not explained by differences in endowments, is that any potential discrimination against disabled workers, as measured by the coefficient effect, is declining. Additionally, this result suggests that one way to combat the rising wage differential is to improve disabled workers' endowments (e.g., greater investments in human capital, or placement in higher-paying occupations or industries). It is also important to note, however, that these improvements appear to be a continuation of a trend rather than any dramatic post-ADA shift.

BENEFIT ANALYSIS

As the percentage of fringe benefits in total compensation continues to increase, benefits become an increasingly important contributor to workers' labor market experience. The CPS allows identification of a worker receiving two fringe benefits from his or her employer: health insurance and a pension plan. The data used for this analysis were obtained from the CPS March supplemental questionnaire and therefore refer to benefit coverage in the years 1980–1999. The probabilities of being included in an employer's pension plan or of receiving health insurance through an employer were fairly stable across the years; however, as Figure 3.3 shows, the proportion of nondisabled workers relative to disabled workers included in a pension plan has grown over the time period.

In 1980, nearly 11 percent more of nondisabled workers were included in a pension plan than disabled workers were. This difference grew to 17 percentage points by 1999. The greater proportion of nondisabled workers receiving either benefit could be closely related to the types of jobs disabled versus nondisabled workers hold. The increase in the difference in proportions could also be related to disabled workers moving into jobs less likely to offer these benefits. For example, Chapter 4 will detail the growth in part-time employment among disabled workers. Neither phenomenon, however, appears to have been impacted by events surrounding the passage and implementation of the ADA. The goal of the analysis of this section is to determine whether

Figure 3.3 Difference in Proportion of Nondisabled and Disabled Workers Receiving Benefits, CPS, 1980–1999

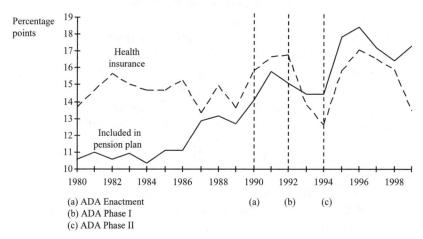

disabled workers are more or less likely than nondisabled workers to be included in their employers' pension plan or to have their employers pay for health insurance, while controlling for all other individual and job characteristics.

Since the observed model is an indicator of coverage/inclusion or not, the empirical model is specified as a probit:

$$(3.9) \quad \tilde{B}_{ij} = Q_i'\omega_j + v_i \quad , \quad v_i \sim N(0,1)$$

where individual i receives benefit j (j = health insurance, pension plan inclusion) if $\tilde{B}_{ij} > 0$. Since $\tilde{B}_{ij}$ is unobserved, a binary variable, $\tilde{B}_{ij}$, is defined as

$$(3.10) \quad B_{ij} = \begin{cases} 1 \\ 0 \end{cases} \text{as } \tilde{B}_{ij} \begin{array}{c} > \\ \leq \end{array} 0.$$

The parameters, ω, are estimated via maximum likelihood probit. Q_i comprises various individual and job characteristics for worker i, including a dummy variable indicating whether the worker is disabled or not. The model is estimated on a sample of workers only; thus, the results are generalizable solely to workers. The marginal effect of being disabled on receiving a benefit is calculated as the partial derivative for each worker, then averaged over the entire sample.[18] The estimation results are depicted in Figure 3.4.[19] A reliable measure of annual earnings is available only since 1987; therefore, the marginal effects only cover the period 1987–1999.[20]

The marginal impact of being disabled on fringe benefit receipt follows the same path for both health insurance and pension plan inclusion: an increasingly *negative* impact of being disabled on the probability of receiving benefits. Since these marginal effects are calculated from specifications which included a control for earnings, the increase cannot be attributed to disabled workers merely being employed in jobs that are lower paying (thus, less likely to offer fringe benefits). The specification also included controls for hours of work (thus the potential impact of part-time employment), occupation, industry, and individual human capital characteristics. While there does seem to be a fairly significant intensification in the negative impact of being disabled in 1995, it would be hard to attribute that to anything other than

**Figure 3.4 Marginal Effect of Disability on the Probability of Fringe
Benefit Receipt, CPS, 1987–1999**

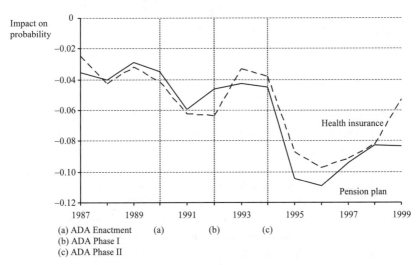

the continuation of a trend, since the negative impact has diminished
somewhat in recent years. However, the negative trend cannot be ignored. There is some evidence that a weakening in 1989 of antidiscrimination laws governing provision of health insurance resulted in
lower rates of benefit incidence among "peripheral" workers, such as
recent hires or those working part-time (Farber and Levy 2000). If
disabled workers fall into the category of "peripheral," this might explain some of the deterioration in health insurance receipt among disabled relative to nondisabled workers.

An additional consideration that might explain the deterioration of
relative health insurance coverage is that the Employment Opportunities for Disabled Americans Act and the Omnibus Budget Reconciliation Act of 1990 amended Title XVI of the Social Security Act to allow
SSI recipients to continue participating in Medicaid (under specific
circumstances) even if their earnings exceeded the SSI qualifying level
(59 FR 41403, 12 August 1994). This amendment became effective in
August 1994. The change would not have typically affected disabled
workers already employed but would have encouraged disabled individuals who previously had not sought employment because of a lack
of health insurance to do so. While this law says nothing about the

provision of pension plans, fringe benefits are highly correlated with one another, so it is not a surprise that as the proportion of disabled workers without employer-provided health insurance increased, the proportion without a pension plan also increased.

CONCLUSIONS

The purpose of this chapter was to evaluate the relative compensation experience of disabled and nondisabled workers over time, and to determine whether any change in that experience is evident in relation to the implementation of the ADA. A pooled, cross-sectional analysis using the CPS data indicated that overall, disabled workers experienced a 3 percent decline in real wages, relative to nondisabled workers, post-ADA, relative to pre-ADA. Results from the SIPP are consistent with the CPS results and show that the wage experience of those with musculoskeletal disabilities is driving that observed wage decline. The real wages of workers with musculoskeletal disabilities declined 4 percent more than for workers without disabilities post-ADA, relative to pre-ADA; workers with other types of disabilities did not experience any different wage change than did nondisabled workers. These results together indicate that overall, the cost of accommodating workers' disabilities exceeds the gain in productivity of those workers. In addition, if accommodating musculoskeletal disabilities results in more costly structural investments, the SIPP results lend support to the theory that wages of disabled workers are sensitive to the degree of accommodation (in terms of cost) required of the employer. This result is consistent with the finding by Gunderson and Hyatt (1996) that firms pass on (through lower wages) the cost of workplace modifications to the hired disabled worker. In light of this, the tax credits in place to assist certain employers in absorbing these costs (Hays 1999) either have not gone far enough or are not being widely used.

In contrast with these overall (disabled versus nondisabled) results, it was found that disabled workers employed by firms covered by the ADA did not experience any wage deterioration relative to disabled workers not covered by the ADA. This combination of results suggests that the wage decline experience by disabled workers relative to nondisabled workers is not the result of explicit accommodation costs being passed on to disabled workers through lower wages (in which case, the wages of covered disabled workers should have deteriorated the most). Rather, all disabled workers seem to be bearing the burden of a perceived additional hiring risk associated with them that may exist post-ADA.

Consistent with the overall relative wage decline identified through the pooled, cross-sectional analysis, further study illustrates that the positive wage differential between disabled and nondisabled workers has risen considerably since 1981. However, the trend does seem to have flattened out since the early 1990s. The large portion of that differential not explained by differences in endowments has also been declining over time, indicating that any potential wage discrimination against disabled workers is at least falling. Additionally, the fact that worker endowments (occupation, education, etc.) contribute positively to the measured wage differential suggests that one way to fight the rising wage differential is to enhance disabled workers' endowments (e.g., greater investments in human capital, or placement in higher-paying occupations or industries).

In addition to the rising wage differentials, the *negative* impact of being disabled on the probability of receiving benefits has also been rising. One potential contributor to this situation is the allowance (as of August 1994) for some disabled workers to continue receiving Medicaid even when their earnings surpass SSI cut-off levels. The combination of the rising wage differential and decreasing probability of disabled workers receiving employer-sponsored health and pension benefits leads to the conclusion that the relative position of disabled workers regarding compensation is deteriorating overall.

The ADA provides a clear mandate "for the elimination of discrimination against individuals with disabilities" (section 2 of the ADA). The evidence provided in this chapter suggests that while potential wage discrimination against the disabled appears to be declining, the improvement is taking place at a very slow rate, and not necessarily as a result of the ADA, as the trend goes back at least to 1981. In addition, even if discrimination is decreasing, the overall compensation experience (including benefit provision) for disabled workers, relative to nondisabled workers, is declining, as well.

Notes

1. See also Burkhauser, Haveman, and Wolfe (1993) for an analysis of the well-being of the disabled.
2. Examples of other applications of this method of analysis can be found in Card (1992), Gruber (1994, 1996), Zveglich and Rodgers (1996), and Hamermesh and Trejo (2000). The reader is reminded of the caveats detailed by Heckman (1996). Also see further discussion in Chapter 2.
3. The first year in the analysis was 1984 due to the poor representation of disabled workers in some occupations in 1983, and since union status was not indicated in 1981 or 1982.
4. While insignificantly different from zero, the coefficient in DeLeire's pooled, cross-sectional analysis was also negative. The results reported in Table 3.1 are robust to defining POST as years past 1990 and to defining POST as 1994 and later.
5. It is important to note that since there is no measure of labor market experience available in the CPS survey, and since disabled workers likely have less labor market experience than nondisabled workers of the same age, the coefficient on the DISABLE dummy variable may be capturing some of the impact of labor market experience on the wage. The inability to control for labor market experience should have a smaller impact, however, on the coefficient for the interaction term of DISABLE $\times$ POST, since the consequence of the absence of an experience variable should be similar across time.
6. See Appendix B for disability types grouped for these classifications.
7. The musculoskeletal grouping includes disabilities of the special senses (e.g., hearing, seeing).
8. See the wage decomposition section in this chapter for details of the procedure used to control for self-selection.
9. Whereas the wages of those with mental disorders did not deteriorate post-ADA, it is of interest to note that the largest (negative) coefficient among types of disability (indicating overall relative wage performance) is that on MENTAL (-0.3427). This is consistent with the findings of Baldwin (1999).
10. The pre and post periods were chosen to achieve balance in the number of years; the results did not change if the number of years were extended.
11. These definitions of "large" and "small" differ from those used in Chapter 2.
12. This specification could also be modified to account for the likely joint determination of wages and hours worked; Moffitt (1984), Lundberg (1985), Altonji and Paxson (1988), and Tummers and Woittiez (1991) all demonstrate the importance of the simultaneous determination of wages and hours. This joint model is not estimated here for simplification, but hours are included as a covariate in the wage equation.
13. Since only 3 percent of the working sample is disabled, nearly all of the coefficient effect is attributed to the disadvantage experienced by the disabled, since the linear combination of the two worlds yields estimates very close to those experienced in the nondisabled world (see Cotton 1988). Other renditions of this

decomposition, such as Oaxaca and Ransom (1994) would result in a similar outcome, since the disabled make up such a small portion of the whole workforce. This same strategy is followed by Baldwin and Johnson (2000) in their analysis of labor market discrimination against disabled workers.

14. The data generating this figure are found in Table C.5 in Appendix C.

15. This finding is consistent with the results reported by Hollenbeck and Kimmel (2001) that people with poor health or disability earn a positive return to education and training, although they find that return to be equal to that of nondisabled individuals.

16. The coefficient of -0.017 on a linear trend estimation had a standard error of 0.0067, making it significantly different from zero at the 95 percent confidence level.

17. The coefficient of 0.006 on a linear trend estimation had a standard error of 0.0027, making it significantly different from zero at the 95 percent confidence level.

18. This is preferable to calculating the marginal benefit for the average person, since we are most likely to be interested in the marginal effect for a worker drawn at random, rather than the marginal effect for the average person in the sample.

19. Table C.6 contains the marginal effects used to generate Figure 3.4.

20. An identical analysis was performed for the entire 1980–1999 time period, excluding the control for earnings. The marginal effect of being disabled was significantly larger, as would be expected, but exhibited the same trend going back to 1980 as that depicted in Figure 3.4.

4

Hours of Work, Distribution, and Representation

In addition to the wage, there are a number of other characteristics that can be used to quantify the *quality* of a worker's job. One feature is whether a job is full-time or part-time. While the availability of part-time employment may be important to disabled workers (and perhaps more so than to nondisabled workers), part-time jobs are often accompanied by lower pay, fewer benefits, and less stability.[1] The first part of this chapter compares and evaluates the *incidence* of part-time employment and *type* of part-time employment (voluntary versus involuntary) across disability status and across time. If disabled workers are considered marginal workers, then they would be more likely to be employed part-time. If, however, disabled part-time workers are more likely to be voluntarily, versus involuntarily, employed part-time, then their part-time status may indicate a greater flexibility that might be needed to accommodate the worker's situation. The chapter then explores the full-time wage premium earned by disabled and nondisabled workers. Disabled workers may not earn as great a premium for committing to a full-time schedule as nondisabled workers. Given the potentially higher fixed cost of accommodating the worker's disability, the individual may have to commit to a greater number of hours before seeing the premium; this could show up in a lower premium at any given definition of part-time employment.[2]

A major characteristic of one's job is its occupation or industry. A popular indicator of the quality of employment of a disadvantaged group is how well that group is represented in desirable occupations relative to some comparison group, and how the disadvantaged group's distribution across occupations compares with that of the comparison group. The occupation that a worker holds, or the industry in which someone works, can play an important role in that person's satisfaction and potential advancement in the labor market. Dual labor market theory suggests that some workers are relegated to undesirable (e.g., low-paying, dead-end) jobs from which they have virtually no escape.[3]

The second part of this chapter will explore the distribution of disabled workers across occupations and industries, relative to the distribution of nondisabled workers, as well as examine the representation of disabled workers in "desirable" jobs. The emphasis will be on how the relative distribution and representation have changed over time and whether the ADA seems to have played a role in their current determination.

HOURS OF WORK

Figure 1.2 in Chapter 1 highlighted a growing disparity in average hours worked per week between disabled and nondisabled workers. This section looks more closely at the role part-time employment plays in that observed decline in hours and determines whether it reflects voluntary or involuntary behavior on the part of disabled workers. Part-time employment among the disabled may not be a sign of marginalization or discrimination because of these individuals' unique physical or mental capabilities and potential income sources. Such employment may be sought by disabled workers (and employers for their disabled workers) as a way to accommodate health limitations. In addition, part-time employment may provide additional earnings that do not jeopardize disability benefits based on income levels.

Incidence of Part-time Employment

Figure 4.1 depicts the percentage of both disabled and nondisabled workers that are employed part-time for each year, 1981 to 2000. Although there is some discrepancy as to the appropriate definition of part-time employment (see Hotchkiss 1991), the CPS definition of "less than 35 hours per week" is retained here. The use of respondent-supplied reasons (later in the chapter) for working less than 35 hours per week makes this the practical choice.

As has been suggested in Chapters 1 and 3, part-time employment has grown among disabled workers between 1981 and 2000 and has declined somewhat among nondisabled workers. By itself, this observation is consistent with the contention that disabled workers are being

Figure 4.1 Percentage of Disabled and Nondisabled Workers That Are Employed Part-Time, CPS, 1981–2000

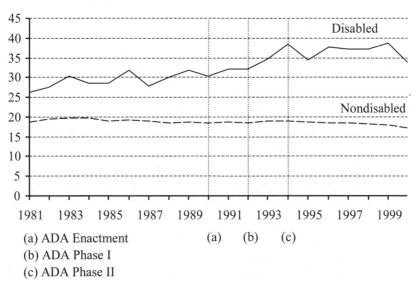

(a) ADA Enactment
(b) ADA Phase I
(c) ADA Phase II

pushed to the fringe and becoming more marginalized. However, these raw numbers do not control for other job or individual characteristics.

In order to appropriately model the impact of having a work-limiting disability on the incidence of part-time employment among workers, a bivariate probit with selection model, as in Chapter 2, is specified. This model estimates the probability of being employed part-time while controlling for unobservable determinants of being both employed and employed part-time. The bivariate specification allows for the two outcomes (employment and part-time employment) to be impacted by the same unobservable factors (e.g., motivation). The selectivity part of the model is merely a recognition that we do not get to see the part-time employment outcome unless the person is employed to begin with, and that those we observe as employed may have systematically different part-time options or make different hours choices than those not employed. Correcting for selectivity allows us to make inferences for anyone from the population, not just those we observe as employed; this is what makes the probability unconditional.

The following model defines the relationship assumed between the employment of person i (EMP$_i$), the probability of being employed part-time (PT_i), and individual characteristics that are believed to affect the employment outcome (X_{1i}) and the incidence of part-time employment (X_{2i}):

(4.1) $EMP_i = \alpha_1 + \gamma'_1 X_{1i} + \beta_1\ DISABLE_i + \epsilon_{1i} = \begin{cases} 1 \text{ if person } i \text{ is employed} \\ 0 \text{ otherwise} \end{cases}$

(4.2) $PT_i = \alpha_2 + \gamma'_2 X_{2i} + \beta_2\ DISABLE_i + \epsilon_{2i}$

$= \begin{cases} 1 \text{ if person } i \text{ is employed part-time} \\ 0 \text{ otherwise.} \end{cases}$

$DISABLE_i$ is equal to 1 if person i is disabled, 0 otherwise; ϵ_{1i} and ϵ_{2i} are distributed as a bivariate normal with means equal to 0, variances equal to 1, and correlation equal to ρ; and α_j, γ_j, and β_j ($j = 1, 2$) are parameter coefficients to be estimated. In addition, of course, PT_i is only observed if $EMP_i = 1$.[4] X_{1i} and X_{2i} include individual demographic characteristics detailed in the notes to Table 4.1. The impact of having a work-limiting disability on part-time employment, then, is determined by calculating the unconditional probability of being employed part-time for each individual, varying the disability index between 0 and 1, then averaging across the sample.[5] Separate specifications are estimated for each year, and the marginal impact of having a work-limiting disability is calculated. The estimation results are depicted in Figure 4.2.[6]

The line in Figure 4.2 reflects an increase in the impact of being disabled on the determinant of the unconditional probability of being employed part-time. A work-limiting disability increased the probability of a worker being observed as employed part-time by 12 percentage points in 2000. This is double the 6 percentage points impact of a disability on being employed part-time estimated for 1981. What is also apparent from the graph is that this effect has experienced a rather consistent upward trend during the entire time period, with the largest adjustment occuring during the ADA phase-in period.

In order to quantify the apparent growth in selectivity-corrected part-time employment among disabled workers, relative to nondisabled workers, the pooled, cross-sectional analysis introduced in Chapter 2 is applied here. The idea behind the analysis is to estimate a cross-sectional, time-series bivariate probit model with dummy variables rep-

Figure 4.2 Impact of Having a Disability on Being Employed Part-Time, CPS, 1981–2000

Percentage-point impact on probability of being disabled

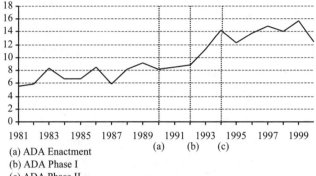

(a) ADA Enactment
(b) ADA Phase I
(c) ADA Phase II

resenting whether the observation shows up in the data pre-ADA or post-ADA and whether the observation is a disabled or nondisabled person. These dummy variables are also interacted to determine whether being disabled had any greater impact on employment after the ADA than before the ADA, relative to the experience of a nondisabled person.[7]

The pooled, cross-sectional analysis looks just like the bivariate probit with selection estimated in one year, except with the additional time-period dummy variables:

$$(4.3) \quad \text{EMP}_i = \alpha_1 + \gamma_1' X_{1i} + \beta_1 \text{ DISABLE}_i + \phi_1 \text{ POST}_i \\ + \theta_1 \text{ DISABLE}_i \times \text{POST}_i + \epsilon_{1i}$$

$$(4.4) \quad \text{PT}_i = \alpha_2 + \gamma_2' X_{2i} + \beta_2 \text{ DISABLE}_i + \phi_2 \text{ POST}_i \\ + \theta_2 \text{ DISABLE}_i \times \text{POST}_i + \epsilon_{2i}.$$

Again, $\text{EMP}_i = 1$ if person i is in the labor force, 0 otherwise, and PT_i is not observed unless $\text{EMP}_i = 1$. DISABLE_i is equal to 1 if person i is disabled, 0 otherwise; POST_i is equal to 1 if person i is observed in 1992 or later (as in Chapter 2); X_{1i} and X_{2i} include individual demographic characteristics; ϵ_{1i} and ϵ_{2i} are distributed as a bivariate normal with means equal to 0, variances equal to 1, and correlation equal to ρ; and ϕ_j and θ_j $(j = 1, 2)$ are additional coefficients to be estimated.

In this framework, the affected group (the disabled) is controlled for by a dummy variable indicating whether the individual has a work-limiting disability, and the time period is controlled for by a dummy variable indicating whether the ADA had been implemented yet or not. Because of the model's nonlinearity, a single parameter coefficient does not tell us the additional impact the ADA had on the difference in employment probabilities between the disabled and nondisabled. Table 4.1 details the regression results.

Using the parameter estimates, the difference in the impact of having a work-limiting disability on part-time employment across the two time periods can be calculated by evaluating the probabilities of interest for each person, varying the DISABLE and POST dummy variables, then taking the difference between these probabilities and averaging those differences across the sample. This calculation translates the

Table 4.1 Employment and Part-Time Employment Bivariate Probit with Selection Results, CPS Combined Years 1981–2000

Regressor	Employment equation	Part-time employment equation
DISABLE = 1	−0.1118***	0.3474***
	(0.0146)	(0.0130)
POST (year = 1992 or later) = 1	−0.0112**	0.0017
	(0.0051)	(0.0037)
DISABLE × POST = 1	−0.0298	0.1775***
	(0.0224)	(0.0190)
Rho	0.7983***	
	(0.0054)	
Log-likelihood	−477,354	
Number of observations	906,646	

NOTE: Regressors included both in the employment and part-time employment equations (but not reported here) include age, education, region, race, gender, marital status, and a central city residence indicator. Regressors unique to the employment equation include the state unemployment rate and the number of weeks worked last year. Regressors unique to the part-time employment equation include occupation and industry dummies, nonlabor income, and a government employer indicator. Standard errors are in parentheses.
*** = significant at the 99 percent confidence level.
** = significant at the 95 percent confidence level.

estimated coefficients from the bivariate probit into a 5 percentage point greater probability of disabled workers being employed part-time than nondisabled workers, post-ADA relative to pre-ADA. In addition, the probability of nondisabled workers being employed part-time changed by less than one-hundredth of a percentage point post- versus pre-ADA.

Type of Part-Time Employment

Given the conclusion that disabled workers are more likely than the nondisabled to be employed part-time and that the disparity is growing, an important consideration is what is the nature of the part-time jobs? Are disabled workers more likely to be employed other than full-time by choice? In order to answer this question, a univariate probit analysis is performed. The purpose of the probit analysis is to determine, among part-time workers, whether the probability of being voluntarily (versus involuntarily) employed part-time has increased or decreased for disabled workers, relative to nondisabled part-time workers, holding constant other factors that may determine the classification.[8] The results of this probit estimation can be found in Figure 4.3.[9] The graph depicts the marginal effect of being disabled on the probability that a part-time worker's status is voluntary. The results are generalizable to part-time workers only. The observation of interest from Figure 4.3 is that prior to 1992, being disabled *decreased* a part-time worker's probability of being voluntarily (versus involuntarily) employed part-time; however after 1992, disabled part-time workers became *more* likely to be voluntarily employed part-time than nondisabled part-time workers. The implication is that much of the growth in part-time employment has been voluntary (for a given set of individual characteristics) and may actually be in response to the better accommodation of a worker's disability.[10]

In order to quantify what may be obvious from Figure 4.3, a pooled, cross-sectional approach is taken to determine the extent to which the disabled are more likely than the nondisabled to be voluntarily employed part-time post-ADA versus pre-ADA. Since this analysis is concerned only with part-time workers as a group, a linear probability model is estimated so that the parameter coefficient is directly interpretable as a marginal effect; again, the results are generalizable only

82   Hotchkiss

Figure 4.3 Impact of Having a Disability on Being Voluntarily Employed Part-Time, CPS, 1981–2000

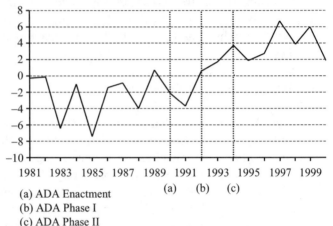

(a) ADA Enactment
(b) ADA Phase I
(c) ADA Phase II

to the part-time employed population. The linear probability model takes the following form:

$$(4.5) \quad \text{VPT}_i = \alpha_3 + \gamma_3' X_{3i} + \beta_3 \text{ DISABLE}_i + \phi_3 \text{ POST}_i$$
$$+ \theta_3 \text{ DISABLE}_i \times \text{POST}_i + \epsilon_{3i}$$

where VPT_i is equal to 1 if person i is voluntarily employed part-time, 0 if involuntarily part-time,
X_i is a set of covariates for each person (individual demographic characteristics),
DISABLE_i is equal to 1 if person i has a work-limiting disability, and
POST_i is equal to 1 if person i is observed in 1992 or later.

In this framework, the affected group (the disabled) is controlled for by a dummy variable indicating whether the individual has a work-limiting disability, and the time period is controlled for by a dummy variable indicating whether the ADA had been implemented yet or not. The coefficient of interest (θ_3), therefore, measures the change in employment probability of disabled workers, relative to nondisabled workers, after implementation of the ADA, relative to before implementation (the other parameter coefficients are analagous to their counterparts in Equations 4.3 and 4.4). X_{3i} includes individual demographic characteristics. Table 4.2 details the regressors included in the estimation and the regression results.

The coefficient on DISABLE × POST confirms that the probability of being voluntarily (versus involuntarily) employed part-time increased 4 percentage points more for disabled part-time workers than for nondisabled part-time workers, post-ADA. This result, taken with the overall growth in part-time employment, suggests that part-time employment and flexible hours may be a mechanism by which employers are able and willing to accommodate workers' disabilities.

Evidence from the SIPP

The pooled, cross-sectional methodologies are appealed to again in order to determine the impact of different types of disabilities on the incidence of part-time employment and on the kind of part-time

Table 4.2 Linear Probability, Voluntary Part-Time Employment Results, CPS Combined Years 1981–2000

Regressor	Coefficient
DISABLE = 1	−0.0158**
	(0.0072)
POST (year = 1992 or later) = 1	−0.0549***
	(0.0023)
DISABLE × POST = 1	0.0401***
	(0.0102)
Adjusted R²	0.08
F statistic	481.91
Number of observations	170,870

NOTE: Observations from 1983 were not included because of the unreliable representation across occupational categories. Regressors included both in the employment and part-time employment equations (but not reported here) include age, education, region, race, gender, marital status, and a central city residence indicator. Regressors unique to the employment equation include the state unemployment rate and the number of weeks worked last year. Regressors unique to the part-time employment equation include occupation and industry dummies, nonlabor income, and a government employer indicator. Standard errors are in parentheses.
*** = significant at the 99 percent confidence level.
** = significant at the 95 percent confidence level.

employment across time using the SIPP data set. The bivariate probit model with selection is estimated with two different specifications. The first includes only a single dummy variable indicator for having a work-limiting disability; the second includes multiple dummies indicating the type of disability a person might have. The general structure of the estimation strategies looks like this:

$$\textbf{(4.6)} \quad \text{EMP}_i = \alpha_1 + \gamma_1' X_{1i} + \sum_{k=(S,I,M,O)}^{n} \beta_1^k \, \text{DISTYPE}_i^k + \phi_1 \, \text{POST}_i$$

$$+ \sum_{k=(S,I,M,O)}^{n} \theta_1^k \, \text{DISTYPE}_i^k \times \text{POST}_i + \epsilon_{1i}$$

$$\textbf{(4.7)} \quad \text{PT}_i = \alpha_2 + \gamma_2' X_{2i} + \sum_{k=(S,I,M,O)}^{n} \beta_2^k \, \text{DISTYPE}_i^k + \phi_2 \, \text{POST}_i$$

$$+ \sum_{k=(S,I,M,O)}^{n} \theta_2^k \, \text{DISTYPE}_i^k \times \text{POST}_i + \epsilon_{2i}$$

where

$$\text{DISTYPE}_i = \begin{cases} \text{DISABLE}_i \text{ in specification 1} \\ \text{MUSCULOSKELETAL}_{i(S)}; \text{ INTERNAL}_{i(I)}; \text{ MENTAL}_{i(M)}; \text{ and} \\ \text{OTHER}_{i(O)} \text{ in specification 2.} \end{cases}$$

Again, $\text{EMP}_i = 1$ if person i is in the labor force and employed, 0 otherwise, and PT_i is not observed unless $\text{EMP}_i = 1$. X_{1i} and X_{2i} include individual demographic characteristics; POST_i is equal to 1 if person i is observed in 1992 or later; DISABLE_i is equal to 1 if person i has a work-limiting disability; MUSCULOSKELETAL_i is equal to 1 if person i has a musculoskeletal disability;[11] INTERNAL_i is equal to 1 if person i has a disability involving the internal systems; MENTAL_i is equal to 1 if person i has a mental disability; OTHER_i is equal to 1 if person i has a disability classified as "other"; and ϵ_{1i} and ϵ_{2i} are distributed as a bivariate normal with means equal to 0, variances equal to 1; and correlation equal to ρ; and α, γ, β, ϕ, and θ are all parameters to be estimated.

   In this framework, the affected group (the disabled) is controlled for by a dummy variable (or set of dummy variables) indicating whether the individual has a work-limiting disability (or type of disability), and the time period is controlled for by a dummy variable indicating whether the ADA had been implemented yet or not. The difference in the impact of having a work-limiting disability on employment across the two time periods can be calculated by evaluating the probabilities of interest for each person, varying the DISTYPE and POST dummy variables, then taking the difference between these probabilities, and averaging across the sample.

An additional estimation is performed on a subsample of part-time workers only to determine whether the type of disability impacts the incidence of voluntary part-time employment. The following equation is estimated via OLS:

$$(\mathbf{4.8}) \quad \mathrm{VPT}_i = \alpha_3 + \gamma_1' X_{3i} + \sum_{k=(S,I,M,O)} \beta_3^k \, \mathrm{DISTYPE}_i^k + \varphi_3 \, \mathrm{POST}_i$$

$$+ \sum_{k=(S,I,M,O)}^{n} \theta_3^k \, \mathrm{DISTYPE}_i^k \times \mathrm{POST}_i + \epsilon_{3i}.$$

Table 4.3 contains the results from estimating both specifications of Equation 4.7 and both specifications of Equation 4.8. The two specifications for each equation correspond to how DISTYPE is defined. Consistent with the findings from the CPS, the results in Table 4.3 indicate that the probability that a disabled worker is employed part-time increased more than the probability for a nondisabled worker, post-ADA relative to pre-ADA. The coefficient of 0.0925 in column 1 of Table 4.3 translates into a relative 2 percentage point greater probability for part-time employment for the disabled post-ADA. In addition, the strongest impact was experienced by those with musculoskeletal (0.1084) and mental (0.1730) disabilities. Regarding voluntary part-time employment, the results suggest that while the impact of having a disability on the probability of being *voluntarily* employed part-time increased post-ADA, that rise was not significantly different from zero for disabled workers as a group. However, those with mental disabilities seem to have experienced a greater increase in the probability of being voluntarily employed part-time than nondisabled part-time workers, post-ADA. This makes sense if mental disorders are the type of disability most effectively accommodated by a flexible or reduced-hours work schedule.[12]

Full-Time Wage Premium

Even beyond whether a part-time job is voluntary or involuntary is the wage penalty experienced by part-time workers. It is well docu-

Table 4.3 Employment and Part-Time Employment Bivariate Probit with Selection and Linear Probability Model for Voluntary Part-Time Employment, SIPP 1986–1997

Regressor	Probability of part-time employment[a]		Probability of voluntary part-time[b]	
	Disability indicator only	Type of disability indicated	Disability indicator only	Type of disability indicated
DISABLE = 1	0.2024*** (0.0188)	—	0.0151 (0.0102)	—
POST (year = 1992 or later) = 1	0.0090 (0.0059)	0.0088 (0.0059)	−0.0380*** (0.0035)	−0.0683*** (0.0038)
DISABLE × POST = 1	0.0925*** (0.0238)	—	0.0095 (0.0127)	—
Musculoskeletal disability = 1	—	0.0821*** (0.0262)	—	−0.0221 (0.0156)
Internal Systems disability = 1	—	0.2743*** (0.0356)	—	0.0275 (0.0194)
Mental disorder disability = 1	—	0.4177*** (0.0464)	—	0.0398* (0.0238)
Other disability = 1	—	0.2587*** (0.0481)	—	0.0414 (0.0261)

MUSCULOSKELETAL × POST = 1	—	0.1084*** (0.0331)	—	0.0238 (0.0195)
INTERNAL × POST = 1	—	−0.0013 (0.0476)	—	0.0068 (0.0258)
MENTAL × POST = 1	—	0.1730*** (0.0550)	—	0.0907*** (0.0281)
OTHER × POST = 1	—	−0.0302 (0.0627)	—	0.0266 (0.0344)
Adjusted R^2	—	—	0.06	0.07
Log-likelihood	−199,110	−199,021	—	—
Number of observations	360,036	360,036	72,890	59,059

NOTE: Standard errors are in parentheses.

*** = significant at the 99 percent confidence level.

** = significant at the 95 percent confidence level.

* = significant at the 90 percent confidence level.

[a]These results are from estimation of a bivariate probit with selection. Other regressors included in the part-time employment equation include age; age squared; nonlabor income; and gender, education, marital status, race, education, region, urban, government, industry, and occupational dummy variables. The selection equation (not reported here) is an employment equation.

[b]These results are from estimation of a linear probability model via OLS and are generalizable to the part-time population only. Other regressors included in the voluntary part-time employment equation include age; age squared; and gender, education, marital status, race, education, region, government, industry, and occupational dummy variables

mented that part-time workers earn considerably less per hour for not making a full-time commitment to his/her employer. This penalty can range from 30 to 60 percent lower wages depending on gender and race groups (Averett and Hotchkiss 1996), and it is a main reason that part-time jobs are considered undesirable (Blank 1990). The reason typically given as to why part-time workers earn a lower wage is the presence of fixed costs associated with hiring personnel. Employers are able to spread these fixed costs over more hours for full-time workers, allowing them to pay higher wages to such individuals. One concern might be that the fixed costs of hiring disabled workers are even greater than for nondisabled workers so that the wage differential between full-time and part-time disabled workers is larger than the differential between full-time and part-time nondisabled workers.

This section presents the full-time/part-time wage differentials experienced by disabled and nondisabled workers, controlling for their selection into the labor market. Standard log wage equations are estimated separately for disabled and nondisabled workers. In the equations for person i, "ft" denotes full-time, and "pt" denotes part-time:

(4.9) $\ln W_{ift} = X_{ift}\beta_{ft} + \epsilon_{ift}$
  $\ln W_{ipt} = X_{ipt}\beta_{pt} + \epsilon_{ipt}$

where $\ln W_i$ is the natural log hourly wage of workers,
  X_i is the explanatory variable,
  β is the set of coefficients to be estimated, and
  ϵ_i is the random error term.

As seen in Chapter 2, there may exist significant self-selection into the labor market, particularly among the disabled population. In order to obtain an estimate of β representative of the population, this selection is controlled for using the standard Heckman (1979) two-step procedure. The first stage of this procedure involves estimating a binary choice model of the following form:

(4.10) $\tilde{Y}_i = Z_i\gamma + u_i$, $u_i \sim N(0,1)$

where Z_i are regressors expected to affect the labor supply decision, γ are parameter coefficients, u_i is the normally distributed random error, and individual i enters the labor force if $\tilde{Y}_i > 0$. Since $\tilde{Y}_i$ is unobserved, a binary variable, Y_i, is defined as

(4.11) $\quad Y_i = \begin{cases} 1 \\ 0 \end{cases}$ as $\tilde{Y}_i \begin{array}{c} > \\ \leq \end{array} 0.$

The parameters, γ, are estimated via maximum likelihood probit, and the inverse Mill's ratio is constructed for inclusion in the wage equations, which are then estimated via OLS. The modified wage equations are

(4.12) $\quad \ln W_{ift} = X'_{ift}\,\beta_{ft} + \delta_{ft}\,\hat{\lambda}_{ift} + v_{ift}$

$\qquad\;\; \ln W_{ipt} = X'_{ipt}\,\beta_{pt} + \delta_{pt}\hat{\lambda}_{ipt} + v_{ipt}$

where X_i and β are defined in Equation 4.9, δ is the coefficient on the selectivity term, v_i is the modified random error term, and all variables are as just defined and $\hat{\lambda}_{ij} = \dfrac{\varphi(Z_{ij}\gamma_j)}{\Phi(Z_{ij}\gamma_j)}$, $j = $ ft, pt.

The parameter estimates that result from OLS estimation of the pair of equations in (4.12) can be used to decompose the wage differential between disabled and nondisabled workers as follows:

(4.13) $\quad \overline{\ln W_{ft}} - \overline{\ln W_{pt}} = \overline{X}'_{ft}\hat{\beta}_{ft} - \overline{X}'_{pt}\hat{\beta}_{pt} + (\hat{\delta}_{ft}\hat{\lambda}_{ft} - \hat{\delta}_{pt}\hat{\lambda}_{pt}).$

The third term on the right-hand side in the parentheses reflects the role differences in selection into the labor market (across part-time status) play in observing differential wages. In order to obtain the selectivity-corrected wage differential, this selectivity term (or difference in selection) is subtracted from the observed wage differential between full-time and part-time workers. This estimation procedure and calculation are performed for each year in the data set to see how different full-time and part-time wages are across disability status and whether that differential has changed over time. If the ADA has forced firms to make environmental changes that also enhance or facilitate a disabled worker's employment, this full-time/part-time wage differential might fall post-ADA. This would be because what used to be an extra fixed cost to hiring a disabled worker has been shifted to general access requirements mandated by other provisions of the ADA.

Figure 4.4 plots these selectivity-corrected full-time/part-time wage differentials for disabled and nondisabled workers across time. Over the entire period, the part-time wage penalty is declining for both disabled and nondisabled workers. After full implementation of the ADA, however, the part-time penalty for disabled workers is less than the part-time wage penalty for nondisabled workers for all but one year. There are two potential explanations for this phenomenon. First, it may be the case that disabled workers are able to negotiate part-time hours in occupations or jobs that would not typically accommodate part-time work arrangements. Second, the situation may reflect a change in social attitude about what is "acceptable" behavior of a committed worker. Either way, a smaller (and shrinking) part-time wage penalty (although still at roughly 40 percent) is good news for disabled workers who may require a shorter workweek to accommodate their impairments.[13]

DISTRIBUTION OF WORKERS

An indication of how mobile workers with disabilities are compared to workers without disabilities (and how this mobility has

Figure 4.4 Full-Time/Part-Time Wage Differentials for Disabled and Nondisabled Workers, CPS, 1981–2000

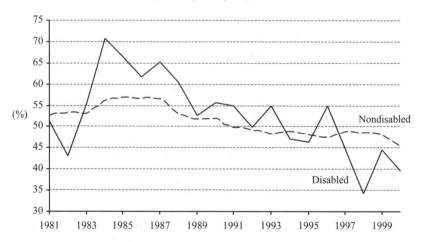

changed over time) is their distribution over different occupations and industries. Figure 4.5 presents the distribution of disabled and nondisabled workers among occupations and industries in 2000. Approximately the same proportions of disabled and nondisabled workers are found in the technical support area and in the farming, fishing, and forestry occupational category. Disabled workers, however, are more heavily concentrated in service and laborer occupations, with nondisabled workers more concentrated in managerial and craft occupations. As we will see later (and as was seen in Chapter 3), this concentration is split along earnings levels, with the occupations in which disabled workers are concentrated being the lower-paying ones. There does not seem to be as wide a disparity in the distribution of workers across industries. However, disabled workers are slightly more concentrated than nondisabled workers in the trade and service industries. Again, these are the lower-paying fields, on average.

Figure 4.5 Distribution of Disabled and Nondisabled Workers across Occupations and Industries, CPS, 2000

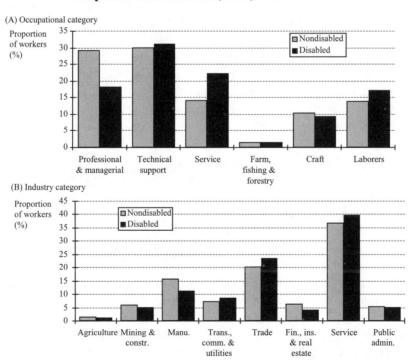

The Duncan Index

The Duncan Index is useful for comparing the distributions of different workers over various occupational and/or industry groups.[14] It can be applied to analyze the distribution of disabled workers in relation to that of nondisabled workers across occupations and industries.

The Duncan Index *(I)* is calculated as follows (Duncan and Duncan 1955):

$$(4.14) \quad I = \frac{1}{2} \sum_{j=1}^{K} \left| \text{ND}_j - \text{D}_j \right|,$$

where K is the total number of occupations or industries and ND_j and D_j are the proportions of all nondisabled and disabled workers, respectively, in occupation or industry j. The index is equal to one-half the sum of the absolute differences between the proportion of nondisabled and disabled persons in each occupation or industry. An index equal to zero means that these groups of workers have identical employment distributions across occupations or industries. An index equal to one corresponds to the extreme situation of complete segregation (no disabled and nondisabled workers in the same occupation or industry). Another way to interpret I is as the percentage of disabled (or nondisabled) workers that would have to change occupations (industries) in order to eliminate the difference in occupational (industry) distributions.

Figure 4.6 presents the Duncan Index calculated for each year and plotted along with the Duncan Index for white and nonwhite groups of workers as a frame of reference.[15] The first noticeable characteristic of these graphs is the growing disparity between the distributions of disabled and nondisabled workers in both occupations and industries. This is in comparison to the declining trend in disparity between nonwhite and white workers. The contrast is particularly interesting since the average occupational index for both disabled versus nondisabled and nonwhite versus white is 0.13, but with very different end points. In other words, an average of 13 percent of disabled or of nondisabled workers would have to change occupations to equalize their distributions across occupations.

**Figure 4.6 Duncan Indices of Dissimilarity across Occupations and
Industries, Disabled versus Nondisabled and Nonwhite versus
White, CPS, 1981–2000**

(A) Occupational dissimilarity

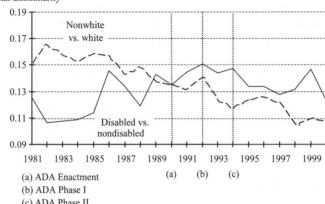

(a) ADA Enactment
(b) ADA Phase I
(c) ADA Phase II

(B) Industry dissimilarity

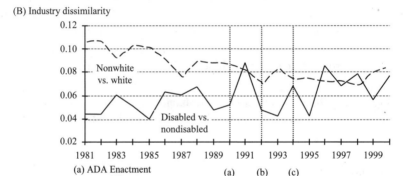

(a) ADA Enactment
(b) ADA Phase I
(c) ADA Phase II

A second observation is that it appears as though the ADA may
have helped to halt the early growth in occupational disparity, since
that series (panel A) seems to have begun a new *downward* trend since
1992 (the first year of implementation of the ADA). This suggests that
disabled workers may be able to take advantage of opportunities not
available to them or that they merely may not have utilized pre-ADA.
To the extent that matching the distribution of nondisabled workers is
an objective, this is a positive outcome for disabled workers.

It is of interest to note that other literature concerned with the distribution of workers may present different goals than equalization of distributions. For example, a dissimilarity in occupational distributions between native and immigrant workers can be considered a positive indicator for an economy, as immigrants fill in occupational gaps left by native workers (see Green 1999). In addition, it may not be clear that the equality of occupational distributions across disability status is desirable. The unique skills and abilities of typical disabled workers may make them fundamentally better suited for occupations not held by the typical nondisabled worker. The growth in disparity among industries does not seem to have followed the pattern of improvement seen among occupations; the distribution of disabled and nondisabled workers has become increasingly disparate, particularly in recent years.

Evidence from the SIPP

Analysis of the SIPP data reveals a similar pattern of growth in the dissimilarity in distributions across occupations between disabled and nondisabled workers. In addition, the SIPP allows for an evaluation of which type of disabilities results in the least similar distribution. Figure 4.7 provides the Duncan Index calculated to compare the distribu-

Figure 4.7 Duncan Indices of Dissimilarity across Occupations and Industries, by Type of Disability, SIPP, 1997

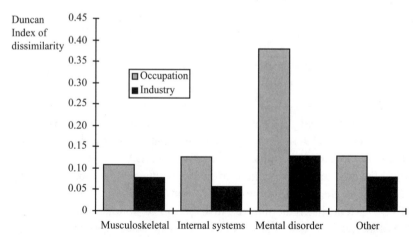

tion of workers with each type of disability with the distribution of nondisabled workers across both occupations and industries. Workers with mental disorders are distributed most differently across both industries and occupations from nondisabled workers: 38 percent of either workers with mental disabilities or nondisabled workers would have to change occupations to equalize the distributions, compared with only 11 percent of workers with a musculoskeletal disability. Workers with mental disorders are much less likely than nondisabled workers to be employed in professional, technical, and craft occupations, whereas they are much more likely to be employed in service and as laborers.

Thirteen percent of workers with mental disorders (or of nondisabled workers) would have to change industries to equalize the distribution, whereas only 6 percent of workers with internal system disabilities would have to switch industries. Workers with mental disorders are less likely to be employed in the transportation, communication, and utility industry, and more likely to be employed in the service industry.

REPRESENTATION OF WORKERS

The equality in the distribution of disabled and nondisabled workers is a goal only if the disparity in distribution reflects characteristics of jobs or industries that are desirable. In other words, if nondisabled workers are systematically more concentrated in jobs that are more attractive than jobs in which disabled workers are concentrated, there is a call to make the distributions more equal. A "share of workers" measure can be used to determine whether disabled workers are more or less concentrated in occupations and industries with appealing qualities, such as higher wages or growth. The desirability of higher wages is obvious, but growth of an occupation could also be considered attractive since it may be indicative of stronger demand for workers, perhaps leading to greater wage growth and occupational advancement.

Representation and Growth

A high-growth indicator for each occupation (and industry) in the sample is constructed as follows:

$$\textbf{(4.15)} \quad \text{HG}_k = \begin{cases} 1 \text{ if } \left(\text{EMP}_k^{t+1} - \text{EMP}_k^t \right) / \text{EMP}_k^t > \\ (1 / K) \sum_{j=1}^{K} \left(\text{EMP}_j^{t+1} - \text{EMP}_j^t \right) / \text{EMP}_j^t \\ 0 \text{ OTHERWISE} \end{cases}$$

where occupation (or industry) k is defined as high-growth if the percentage change in employment between year t and $t + 1$ for that occupation exceeds the average percentage change in employment in all occupations represented in the sample (K corresponds to the total number of occupations or industries). The probability of being employed in a high-growth occupation (and/or industry) is determined as a function of individual characteristics, including disability status.

The sample was split into three time periods, and the employment growth of each occupation and industry represented in the sample was determined by a source external to the data file.[16] Table 4.4 contains the growth rates of each occupation and industry represented in the sample. For example, for the 1983–1989 period, service occupations, managerial and professional specialty, and technical, sales, and administrative support are considered "high growth," since their growth exceeds the average for all occupations. Similarly, for the same period, mining and construction; transportation and public utilities; retail trade; finance, insurance, and real estate; services; and public administration are all considered high-growth industries.

Simple probit models were estimated to determine whether disabled workers are more or less likely to be employed in growing occupations or industries:

$$\textbf{(4.16)} \quad \tilde{Y}_i = X_i \beta_j + \epsilon_i, \qquad \epsilon_i \sim \text{N}(0,1)$$

where individual i's job is in a growing occupation/industry if $\tilde{Y}_i > 0$. Since $\tilde{Y}_i$ is unobserved, a binary variable, Y_{ij}, is defined as

$$\textbf{(4.17)} \quad Y_{ij} = \begin{cases} 1 \\ 0 \end{cases} \text{ as } \hat{Y}_{ij} \overset{>}{\underset{\le}{}} 0.$$

The set of parameters, β, were estimated via maximum likelihood probit. X_i comprises various individual and job characteristics for

Table 4.4 Employment Growth Rates for Industry and Occupational Classifications

	Growth rate (%)		
	1983–89	1987–93	1991–98
Occupation			
Managerial and professional specialty	28.8	16.2	25.9
Technical, sales, and administrative support	15.6	5.6	6.1
Service	12.3	11.7	9.7
Precision production, craft, and repair	12.1	−1.0	8.8
Operators, fabricators, and laborers	12.0	−0.8	4.6
Farming, forestry, and fishing	−7.5	−3.6	−0.1
Average Growth Rate	**12.2**	**4.7**	**9.2**
Industry			
Agriculture	−9.7	−2.9	3.3
Mining and construction	18.8	−3.9	16.1
Manufacturing	8.6	−5.8	0.7
Transportation and public utilities	15.8	8.2	13.0
Wholesale and retail trade	14.6	7.5	11.4
Finance, insurance, and real estate	22.7	2.7	10.2
Services	23.6	17.7	18.4
Public administration	17.9	10.2	4.1
Average growth rate	**14.0**	**4.2**	**9.7**

SOURCE: Author's calculations from Jacobs (1998).

worker i, including a dummy variable indicating whether the worker is disabled or not. The model was estimated on a sample of workers only; therefore, the results are generalizable to workers only. The marginal effect of disability on being employed in a high-growth occupation or industry was calculated as the marginal benefit for each worker, then averaged over the entire sample. Table 4.5 presents the estimated marginal effects of a work-limiting disability on having a job in a high-growth occupation or industry.

In each of the three years analyzed, the probability of a disabled worker being employed in a high-growth occupation was from 2 to 5 percentage points less than the probability of a nondisabled worker being employed in a high-growth occupation. In addition, the marginal (negative) effect was the highest during the post-ADA years, suggesting that the ADA has not improved the opportunity of disabled workers to move into high-growth occupations. On the other hand, disabled

Table 4.5 Marginal Effect of Disability on the Probability of Employment in a "High Growth" Occupation or Industry, CPS

Year	∂PROB (HIGH GROWTH OCCUPATION)/∂DISABLE	∂PROB (HIGH GROWTH INDUSTRY)/∂DISABLE
1989	−0.0299	0.0123
	(0.0092)	(0.0108)
1993	−0.0194	0.0469
	(0.0085)	(0.0121)
1998	−0.0453	0.0261
	(0.0140)	(0.0129)
All three years	−0.0381	0.0268
	(0.0068)	(0.0070)

NOTE: Probit estimations included the following regressors, in addition to a disability dummy variable: age; age squared; regional, education, marital, female, and nonwhite dummy variables; and occupation (for the industry probit) and industry (for the occupation probit) dummy variables. Standard errors are in parentheses.

workers have been more likely to be employed in high-growth *industries*. Unfortunately, a worker's industry does not reflect as much on an individual's job opportunities as one's occupation does. For example, for someone with skills suited to a secretarial job, a decline in manufacturing as an industry is not as devastating to the person's opportunities as a decline in the administrative support occupation. Of course, occupational representation within an industry, such as the proportion of those in the precision production occupation in manufacturing industry, could be an important consideration.

Representation and High Wages

A simple correlation between wages in an industry or occupation and the percentage of workers in that industry or occupation that are disabled was performed to determine whether disabled workers are concentrated in low-paying occupations. The wage decomposition results in Chapter 3 suggest that disabled workers are concentrated in the lower-paying occupations and industries, since occupation and industry regressors contribute positively and significantly to the observed wage differential between disabled and nondisabled workers.

Figure 4.8 plots this correlation coefficient for each year for both occupations and industries. First, over the entire time period, the corre-

**Figure 4.8 Correlation Coefficients, Concentration of Disabled Workers
and Industry/Occupation Wage, CPS, 1981–2000**

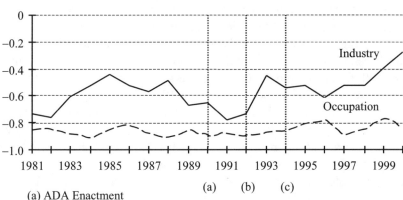

(a) ADA Enactment
(b) ADA Phase I
(c) ADA Phase II

NOTE: Correlation coefficients plotted include projections for industry years 1984 and
1999 and occupation year 1983, as these coefficients appeared to be extreme
outliers.

lation coefficient between concentration of disabled workers in an occupation and the average hourly wage in that occupation is -0.82;
the average across industries is -0.55. Disabled workers are more
concentrated in the low-wage occupations and industries. Consequently, concern about the disparity in distributions across occupations
and industries is warranted. While not particularly dramatic, there appears to be some modest improvement (becoming less negative) in
these correlation coefficients since 1992 (the first year of ADA implementation). If the ADA did enhance the mobility of disabled workers
across occupations and industries, it appears as though these individuals are moving slightly toward the more desirable jobs, in terms of
wage levels.

CONCLUSIONS

This chapter explored some dimensions of employment not captured merely by employment probabilities or overall compensation.
Initially, the incidence of and type of part-time employment were com-

pared across disability status. Then, the distribution of disabled workers relative to nondisabled workers across occupations and industries was analyzed. Finally, the representation of disabled workers in what might be considered "desirable" occupations was evaluated.

Having a work-limiting disability increased the probability of a worker being observed as employed part-time by 12 percentage points in 2000; this is double the 6-percentage-point impact of a disability on being employed part-time estimated for 1981. The upward trend in the relative occurrence of part-time employment among disabled workers does seem to have gotten a boost during the phase-in period of the ADA. There also seems to have been an ADA-related shift in the type of part-time employment experienced by disabled workers. After 1992, disabled part-time workers went from being less likely voluntarily employed part-time to more likely relative to nondisabled part-time workers. The implication is that much of the growth in part-time employment has been voluntary and may actually reflect the required accommodation of a worker's disability. Analysis with the SIPP data indicates that the growth in part-time employment has occurred primarily among those with musculoskeletal and mental disabilities, but that only part-time workers with mental disabilities have experienced any significant relative increase in *voluntary* part-time employment. This may reflect the fact that part-time or flexible work hours may be the best and least costly way to accommodate a worker with a mental disorder.

An additional indication that part-time jobs are becoming an acceptable alternative for employing disabled workers is the greater decline between 1981 and 2000 in the full-time/part-time wage differential among disabled workers than among nondisabled workers. In 2000, full-time nondisabled workers earned a wage (*ceteris paribus*) 45 percent higher than part-time nondisabled workers, while the full-time/part-time wage differential between disabled workers was only 39 percent. It may also be the case that required accommodation enables disabled workers to negotiate part-time hours on a job that would not normally allow for flexible hours. Either of these reasons translates into an improved labor market experience for disabled workers in the dimension of hours of work.

The movement of nondisabled workers away from part-time employment and the movement of disabled workers towards part-time employment may be one explanation why we observe a growing disparity in the distribution of workers across occupations (and industries). It may be the case that some occupations, such as service occupations, are better suited to accommodate workers with disabilities. Workers with mental disorders are the most dissimilar in their distribution across both occupations and industries as compared with workers without disabilities. This might be expected considering that workers with mental disorders are the most likely to be voluntarily moving into part-time employment, which may mean that they are restricted in the types of occupations or industries open to this type of accommodation. The overall growth in occupational distributional disparity, however, is mitigated somewhat post-1992. This may mean that, post-ADA, disabled workers have been able to profit from opportunities not previously available to them or that they merely may not have taken advantage of pre-ADA.

To the extent that occupations and industries in which nondisabled workers are concentrated are desirable, this mitigation of dissimilarity since 1992 is a positive outcome for disabled workers. Further analysis found that in each of the three years analyzed, nondisabled workers were more likely to be employed in high-growth occupations and in the highest-paying occupations and industries. Consequently, concern about the disparity in distributions across occupations and industries is warranted, since nondisabled workers seem to be more concentrated in what might be considered desirable occupations and industries than are disabled workers. On the upside, there does appear to be modest movement of disabled workers into more high-paying occupations and industries since 1992.

Notes

1. See Averett and Hotchkiss (1995, 1996, and 1997), Hotchkiss (1991), and Farber and Levy (2000).
2. This phenomenon, identified by Averett and Hotchkiss (1996), has been the experience of women in the labor market.
3. For a discussion of labor market segmentation and dual labor market theory and references to this literature, see Kaufman and Hotchkiss (2000, Chapter 6).
4. The bivariate probit model with selection gives rise to the following likelihood function:

$$\ln L = \sum_{\text{EMP}=1,\,\text{PT}=1} \log \Phi_2 \left[\gamma_1' X_{1i}, \gamma_2' X_{2i}, \rho \right]$$
$$+ \sum_{\text{EMP}=1,\,\text{PT}=0} \ln \Phi_2 \left[\gamma_1' X_{1i}, \, -\gamma_2' X_{2i}, \rho \right] + \sum_{\text{EMP}=0} \ln \Phi \left[-\gamma_1' X_{1i} \right],$$

where Φ_2 is the bivariate normal cumulative distribution function and Φ is the univariate normal cumulative distribution function.

5. This method of calculating the marginal effect of a change in a dummy variable is referred to as a measure of discrete change and is described in greater detail by Long (1997, pp. 135–138).

6. Table C.7 (column 1) in Appendix C contains the marginal effects used to generate Figure 4.2.

7. This type of pooled, cross-sectional analysis has been applied by many researchers (for example, Card 1992; Gruber 1994 and 1996; Zveglich and Rodgers 1996; and Hamermesh and Trejo 2000). The technique, however, also has its critics (such as Heckman 1996). The primary criticism of this pooled, cross-sectional approach is that it is impossible to control for unobserved changes in the environment that occurred at the same time as the event of interest. Issues of potential concern in this regard are explored in Chapter 2.

8. Voluntary part-time is defined as (1994–2000) working less than 35 hours per week and did not want to work full-time, and (1981–1993) reason for working less than 35 hours per week coded as 07–15 (see Stratton 1994 for justification). Category reasons 07–15 are holiday, labor dispute, bad weather, own illness, on vacation, too busy with school or house, did not want to work full-time, full-time work week is less than 35 hours, or other.

9. Table C.7 (column 2) in Appendix C contains the marginal effects used to generate Figure 4.3.

10. These results are consistent with those of Schur (2002), who finds that part-time and contingent work grows among the disabled during tight labor markets (where demand is strong relative to supply), which would be expected if these arrangements are voluntary.

11. The musculoskeletal category includes disabilities of the special senses (e.g., hearing, seeing).

12. See Magill (1997) for a detailed discussion about how flexible and part-time work schedules can often serve as low- or no-cost solutions to the accommodating problem. However, indirect costs, such as having to hire additional workers to cover lost hours of a disabled part-time worker, should not be ignored.

13. The SIPP data showed the same differential decline for both disabled and nondisabled workers as seen in the CPS data, but essentially inconsequential differences across disability status in any given year.

14. An additional distribution index, the IP Index (see Watts 1992), was also evaluated, and the conclusions were the same. While there is a direct mathematical relationship between these two indices, the IP index reflects the percentage of workers in the labor market that would have to switch occupation or industry in order to equalize the distribution of disabled and nondisabled workers across occupations or industries, while maintaining the original occupational structure. Since the conclusions were the same regardless of the index employed, the more familiar Duncan Index is detailed here.

15. The actual indices plotted in Figure 4.6 are contained in Table C.8 in Appendix C. The indices calculated for the distribution across industries are consistent with

what Yelin and Cisternas (1996) calculated using the National Health Interview Survey; their data indicate that the relative distributions of disabled and nondisabled workers have been fairly steady as far back as 1970. The occupational categories in their data were not comparable to those in the CPS, however.

16. Employment growth was calculated as the percentage change in the number of workers in an occupation from one time period to the next.

5

Separation, Unemployment, and Job Search

Separation from one's job is an important dimension of the experience of a worker. If separations are dominated by involuntary actions, such as a layoff or being fired, the worker's experience is obviously diminished. Voluntary separation, however, may or may not be an indicator of a positive situation. On the one hand, voluntary separation (quitting) may indicate that workers are able to respond to better job opportunities through labor market mobility. On the other hand, excessive voluntary separations may reflect instability among that group of workers. This may be of particular importance for disabled workers who may need to voluntarily quit jobs for health reasons. The first analysis in this chapter considers a group of labor force participants who have experienced a recent job separation and evaluates the determinants, including disability status, of the type of separation.[1]

Unemployment is another important dimension of the labor market experience. In a given month in 2000, an average of 3.3 million people flowed into unemployment.[2] Between the ages of 18 and 27, individuals average 4.4 unemployment spells and spend an average of 31 weeks unemployed (Veum and Weiss 1993). In addition, Figure 5.1 shows that, in 1999, workers in the CPS data used here spent from roughly one to two weeks on average looking for work.[3] Figure 5.1 also shows that while the disabled clearly spend more of their time in a given year looking for work, the movement of weeks spent in this activity essentially mirrors the trend for the nondisabled. The next sections will look more closely at this time spent looking for work.

Job separation is only one reason why a worker might be unemployed. Workers entering the labor market for the first time and rejoining the labor market after an absence are also considered unemployed until they find a job. Examining the composition of the unemployed over time can tell us something about flows into and out of the labor market. The second analysis of this chapter will explore the probabilities of unemployment categories as a function of disability status.

Figure 5.1 Weeks Spent Looking for Work, by Disability Status, CPS, 1980–1999

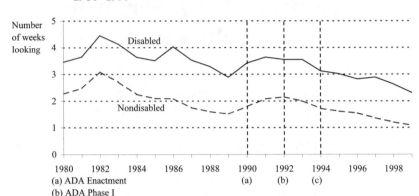

The worker's situation while unemployed, namely the job search experience, will also be explored in this chapter. For the same reasons argued in Chapter 2, one would expect that disabled workers would have a more difficult time finding a job that suits their skills, and would thus have longer spells of search duration, *ceteris paribus*. In addition, if disabled workers are subjected to hiring discrimination, search duration would also increase. The third analysis in this chapter will evaluate the search spells of disabled and nondisabled workers and determine whether differential search strategies are more successful for one group or the other.

SEPARATION

If disabled workers have a more difficult time finding employment or employers that will accommodate their disabilities, they may experience greater voluntary turnover as they continue to search for the job that will best match their skills. On the other hand, the fear of losing one's health benefits ("job-lock") may be more severe for disabled workers, leading to fewer voluntary separations relative to nondisabled workers (see Kapur 1998; Buchmueller and Valletta 1996). The impact of the ADA on voluntary separations among the disabled is ambiguous. Voluntary separations may increase as more opportunities become available to disabled workers, but may also decrease as employers make disability accommodations, which have been shown to increase tenure and reduce voluntary turnover among disabled workers (Burkhauser, Butler, and Kim 1995).

If disabled workers suffer from discrimination, or overall have less labor market experience or tenure with their employers, they might suffer more frequent involuntary separations through layoffs. Based purely on anecdotal evidence, Yelin (1991) concludes that "persons with disabilities, like those from minority races, constitute a contingent labor force, suffering displacement first [as an industry declines]" (p. 135). However, if disabled workers are a more selected group in the sense that they are less substitutable with other inputs (perhaps the accommodations employers have made for them enhance their productivity beyond that of nondisabled workers, *ceteris paribus*), they will be less likely to be laid off as marginal workers. In other words, the discrimination or marginalization might be taking place at the hiring stage, rather than at the separation stage of the relationship. The passage of the ADA might decrease involuntary separations among disabled workers if employers are fearful of accusations of discrimination.

Among workers who have separated from their jobs, the CPS contains information about why a separation occurred. Figure 5.2 presents the percentage of disabled and nondisabled individuals who have experienced a recent job separation and the reason for that separation. The series are split into pre- and post-1994, since the universe for the job separation question changed at that time.[4] Overall, disabled workers have a greater incidence of voluntary separations, and nondisabled workers have a greater incidence of involuntary separations. The break in 1994 makes it difficult to draw any conclusions regarding trends. In order to look more closely at any possible trends, and to control for individual characteristics, a multinomial logit estimation was performed.[5] A multinomial logit specification allows us to specify multiple possible outcomes (e.g., separation types) as a function of a variety of observed characteristics and unobservable factors, recognizing that as one's probability of having separated voluntarily increases, the probability of having separated involuntarily necessarily decreases.

Job separations have been divided into three categories: 1) voluntary separation, 2) involuntary separation, and 3) "other" separation.[6]

**Figure 5.2 Percentage of Job Separations by Type and Disability Status,
CPS, 1981–2000**

(A) Voluntary separations

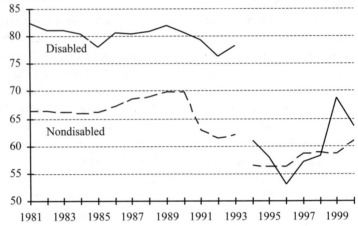

(B) Involuntary separations

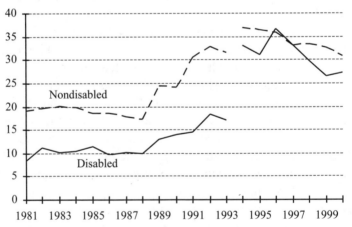

The separation is modeled as a multinomial logit, where the probability of observing a job separation (S) of type j for person i is equal to

(5.1) $P_j = P(S_i = j), j = 1,2,3.$

(5.2) $\dfrac{P_j}{P_j + P_3} = F(\beta_j'X)$ for $j = 1,2,$

where $F(\cdot)$ is a cumulative distribution function, X corresponds to characteristics expected to influence the type of separations, and β_j dictates *how* those characteristics affect separation j.

This means

(5.3) $\dfrac{P_j}{P_3} = \dfrac{F(\beta_j'X)}{1 - F(\beta_j'X)} = G(\beta_j'X)$ for $j = 1,2.$

Because of the rules of summation:

(5.4) $P_3 = 1/\left[1 + \displaystyle\sum_{j=1}^{2} G(\beta_j'X)\right]$ and $P_j = \dfrac{G(\beta_j'X)}{1 + \displaystyle\sum_{j=1}^{2} G(\beta_j'X)}.$

If we let

(5.5) $G(\beta_j'X) = \exp(\beta j'X)$ and Y_{ij}

$= \begin{cases} 1 \text{ if person } i \text{ falls in separation category } j \\ 0 \text{ otherwise} \end{cases},$

the log likelihood function $(\ln L)$ can be written as

(5.6) $\ln L = \displaystyle\sum_{i=1}^{3}\sum_{j=1}^{3} Y_{ij} \ln P_{ij},$

where $P_{ij} = \dfrac{\exp(X_i'\beta_j)}{1 + \displaystyle\sum_{k=1}^{2} \exp(X_i'\beta_k)}$ and $P_{i3} = \dfrac{1}{1 + \displaystyle\sum_{k=1}^{2} \exp(X_i'\beta_k)}.$

The multinomial logit gives three sets of parameter estimates, each set describing the probability of one of the separation types. Each person has a probability of every type of separation, and those three probabilities sum to one (since the sample contains only those who experienced a separation). Figure 5.3 summarizes the marginal effects of having a work-limiting disability on the probability that the separation was involuntary or voluntary for years 1981–2000.[7]

Over the period, the probability of a separation being voluntary is, on average, 12 percentage points higher for workers with disabilities, relative to workers without disabilities. This result lends support for the theory that disabled workers may have more difficulty finding the right "match," and are therefore more likely to quit in search of a better accommodation for their disability. It could also point to the higher frequency of health-related quits among the disabled. In addition, with the exception of the most recent two years, the impact of disability on voluntary turnover seems to be declining since the phase-in of the ADA. This suggests that mandated accommodations relieve the disabled worker of the burden of changing jobs in order to search for a better fit; the worker's current job (or employer) does the changing to better suit the disabled worker. It could also mean that employers are accommodating potential health cycles that in the past would

Figure 5.3 Marginal Effect of Being Disabled on the Probability of Separation Type, CPS, 1981–2000

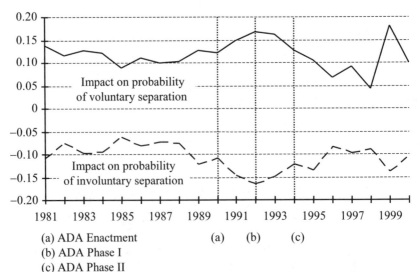

(a) ADA Enactment
(b) ADA Phase I
(c) ADA Phase II

have necessitated a job separation. This result is marginally consistent with the research of Baldwin and Schumacher (1999), who find, using 1990 data from the SIPP, that disabled workers are more likely (but insignificantly so) to voluntarily separate from their employers, relative to nondisabled workers.

The probability of a separation being involuntary is, on average over the time period, 11 percentage points *lower* for workers with disabilities. This does not support the notion that disabled workers are considered "marginal." Since this negative impact of being disabled on involuntary separations is in evidence well before the ADA, it may also help alleviate employers' fears that the ADA makes it more "difficult" to dismiss disabled workers, on average. These results are not consistent with these of Baldwin and Schumacher (1999), who find that disabled workers are slightly *more* likely to experience an involuntary separation than nondisabled workers. Baldwin and Schumacher (1999) explore overall job turnover, where nonseparation plays a large role in the outcomes of workers analyzed; their results are primarily driven by the fact that disabled workers experience more separations overall. The analysis here compares only *types* of separation and does not consider the nonseparation outcome. This approach is more relevant when considering the separation experience of workers, rather than the question of turnover. In other words, the question answered here is, "Among those who have separated, what is the most common reason?"

Further evidence that disabled workers are not marginalized is the experience during the recession of the early 1990s. Separation during the early nineties for disabled workers was even less likely to be the result of involuntary action, relative to nondisabled workers, compared with the years prior to and since the recession.

UNEMPLOYMENT

Examining the composition of the unemployed over time can tell us something about flows into and out of the labor market. For example, if most of the unemployed are new entrants or reentrants, these individuals would constitute an inflow of workers into the labor market. In 2000, job losers (fired or laid-off) made up the largest category of all the unemployed (44 percent), and re-entrants represented the next largest category (36 percent of the unemployed).[8] As far as disabled workers are concerned, a policy such as the ADA is expected to decrease the cost of entering the labor market (with improved accommodation and fewer barriers to employment), thus potentially increasing the incidence of new entrants and reentrants to the labor market, relative to these categories for nondisabled workers.

Another multinomial logit was estimated to evaluate the determinants of unemployment categories, with the type of unemployment divided into four classifications: 1) job loser (fired or laid-off), 2) job leaver (quit), 3) reentrant to the labor force, and 4) new entrant to the labor force. The first two categories were considered in detail in the previous section. The focus of the analysis in this section is on the relative probabilities that unemployment spells for disabled workers are of the new entrant or reentrant variety, and on whether the composition of the unemployed was altered by the ADA. The structure of the multinomial logit estimated for this analysis is the same as described by Equations 5.1 through 5.5, except that there are four categories instead of just three.

The multinomial logit provides four sets of parameter estimates. Each set describes the probability of one of the unemployment types; every person has a probability of each type of unemployment, and those four probabilities sum to one (since the sample contains only those who are unemployed). The CPS started categorizing types of unemployment in 1989, so that is the first year of analysis. The four panels in Figure 5.4 summarize the predicted probabilities of the jobless experiencing each of the categories of unemployment.[9] The actual probabilities have been smoothed using a third-order polynomial.[10] The smoothing process amounts to taking a plotted series and drawing a smooth line through the middle of the plotted points. The effect is to highlight any trends that are more difficult to decipher from the raw data. The higher the order of the polynomial (e.g., third- versus first-order), the more changes in direction will be captured (the higher the order, the less restrictive is the smoothing).

The probabilities of being a job loser (fired or laid-off) and a job leaver (quit) are consistent with the results reported for separations in the previous section (see Figures 5.2 and 5.3). The disabled are less likely to be job losers than the nondisabled (panel A) and (typically) more likely to be job leavers (panel B). The disabled unemployed are

Figure 5.4 Probability of Different Types of Unemployment by Disability Status, CPS, 1989–2000

(A) Unemployed is a job loser

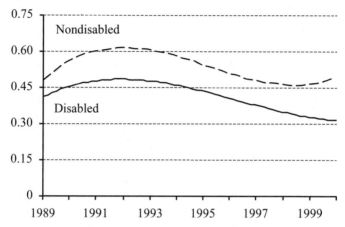

(B) Unemployed is a job leaver

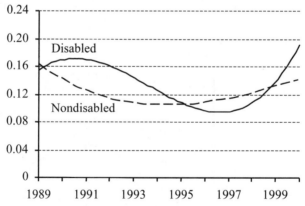

also predicted to be more likely to be new entrants and reentrants into the labor market (panels C and D) than the nondisabled. This indicates that the disabled move into and out of the labor market more than do nondisabled workers. This is not good news for the disabled, as shifts between jobs (even with intervening unemployment) typically result in better subsequent outcomes than movements out of and back into the labor market (Horvath and Shack 1986).

Figure 5.4 (continued) Probability of Different Types of Unemployment by Disability Status, CPS, 1989–2000

(C) Unemployed is a new entrant

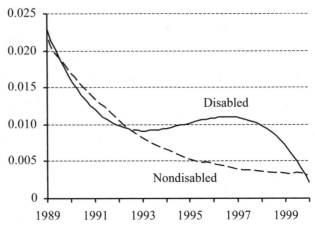

(D) Unemployed is a reentrant

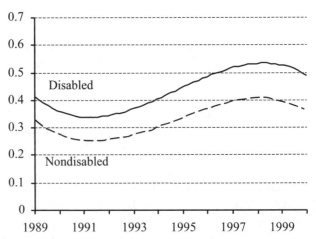

There does not seem to be any noticeable effect of the passage and phase-in of the ADA on the probability of unemployed disabled workers being in one category of unemployment or another. There is an upswing in the probability of being a reentrant beginning about 1992, but that change is shared by the nondisabled, which likely means it was a general labor market response (by all workers) of recovery from the early 1990s recession; workers discouraged by the recession began to reenter the labor market as the economy recovered. The fairly steady decline in the probability of being a job loser among disabled workers since 1993 deviates somewhat from that observed for nondisabled workers, perhaps signaling that additional accommodations have made disabled workers even that much less marginalized than before. It could also be signaling employers' fears of being accused of inappropriately dismissing disabled workers. Perhaps, because of these fears, employers are even more scrutinizing when hiring a disabled worker, improving the chances of a good fit.

JOB SEARCH

The theory proposed so far as to why the disabled have a lower probability (among those who separate) of being a job loser, or experiencing an involuntary separation, is that employers are more careful in their hiring of disabled workers. Employers may feel that hiring a disabled worker is more risky, or they may fear the consequences if they would have to dismiss the worker. The greater "care" in hiring a disabled worker should show up in longer search spells. Of course, the observation of longer search spells is also consistent with a theory of discrimination against disabled workers, but it is *necessary* to provide support for the preceding theory. Figure 5.5 presents the average difference between the expected search spells of disabled workers and of nondisabled workers.[11] While exhibiting some degree of variation from year to year, the average length differential ranges from a high of 24 weeks in 1987 to a low of 0.66 weeks in 1998. The median spell length differential (not controlling for any individual characteristics) for the entire time period is approximately 14 weeks.[12]

The expected impact of the ADA on search spell length of disabled workers is ambiguous. The legislation may reduce search spells by

Figure 5.5 Average Search Spell Length Differential between Unemployed Disabled and Nondisabled Searchers, CPS, 1981–2000

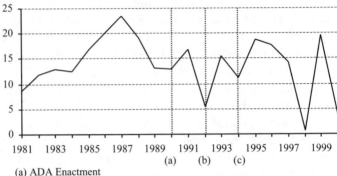

Number of weeks

(a) ADA Enactment
(b) ADA Phase I
(c) ADA Phase II

making overt hiring discrimination more difficult. It may also shorten spells merely by raising the awareness of employers to the capabilities of workers with disabilities. On the other hand, it may lengthen search spells if the fear of dismissing disabled workers is so great that employers increase their scrutiny of such individuals before hiring them. It appears from Figure 5.5 that the ADA did not have an impact on the average search spell length differential. Fitting a trend line through the data points in Figure 5.5 results in a zero slope; while there is a wide variation in the average from year to year, and while the difference does not exhibit any trend, it is positive throughout the time period.

Search Duration Estimation

The difficulty of estimating job search spells using CPS data is notorious (Kiefer, Lundberg, and Neumann 1985). Individuals who are currently searching for a job are asked how long they have been searching, so that everyone in the sample is in the middle of a censored spell. Akerlof and Main's (1981) approach to using CPS data is to double the observed censored search spells and then treat them as completed. This results in an accurate representation of completed search spells under the assumption of a steady state.[13] Under this assumption, the impact of various demographic characteristics on the length of a search spell can be determined. The demographic of particular interest, of course, is whether someone has a work-limiting disability. The accelerated failure time model that will be described allows for the estimation of these spell lengths, taking into account how long someone has already been searching. This is of interest if, for example, the longer someone has been searching the harder it is for him or her to escape the search (by finding a job).

If a person has a completed search spell length, t, the contribution to likelihood is $f(t)$, where $f(.)$ is the probability density function of the random search duration, T. In order to describe the variation in T conditional on a set of explanatory variables, X, a specific distribution is specified for T as a function of a set of parameters, β. If T_0 is a random time duration sampled from the baseline distribution for an individual whose covariates are all zero, then for nonzero covariates, X, the event time will be $T(X) = \exp(X'\beta)T_0$ (see Kalbfleisch and Prentice 1980; Kiefer 1988). This model specification allows writing the log duration as a linear function of the covariates, $\ln t = X'\beta + \sigma\epsilon$. Assuming T is distributed as a Weibull, the following likelihood function results:

$$(5.7) \quad L(\beta|t_i,X_i) = \prod_i \frac{1}{\sigma} g((\ln t_i - X_i'\beta)/\sigma),$$

where $g(.)$ is the probability density function of the transformed search duration; in this case, $g(.)$ takes on the form of an extreme value distribution. Regressors for the duration analysis include age; age squared; nonlabor income; female, single, nonwhite, education, and regional dummies; dummy variables for availability for employment, whether searcher wanted a full-time job, and whether searcher worked last year; and dummy variables for search methods, disability status, and search methods interacted with disability status.

The specification of a duration model, as opposed to merely estimating the relationship by OLS, for example, allows for the likelihood that the chance of a search spell ending in time t is related to how large t is (i.e., the probability that someone finds a jobs and stops searching in t depends on how long the individual has already been searching).

This relationship between the chances of finding a job and how long a worker has been searching is referred to as duration dependence.

Figure 5.6 plots the predicted expected search duration for the total sample, by disability status, for each year.[14] Over this entire time period, on average, disabled individuals could expect to be looking for a job 3.2 weeks longer than nondisabled workers with identical demographic characteristics and search strategies. The only trends that appear in this graph correspond to the general conditions of the labor market; predicted expected duration for both disabled and nondisabled searchers moves together. There is an obvious rise in search length beginning in the early nineties (corresponding to the recession of the period), and duration begins to fall again in the mid 1990s.

Controlling for demographic and search strategy reduces the average marginal effect of being disabled on expected duration over this time period from approximately 14 weeks to approximately 3 weeks. The implication is that the majority of the observed search duration differential is explained by demographic and search strategy differences. This suggests that discrimination in hiring may not be of great concern, but it does not rule out that employers are more "careful" in screening disabled workers. In other words, it is possible that the characteristics of disabled and nondisabled workers are being valued equally, but that employers go to greater length to discern the fit of a

Figure 5.6 Predicted Expected Search Duration by Disability Status, CPS, 1981–2000

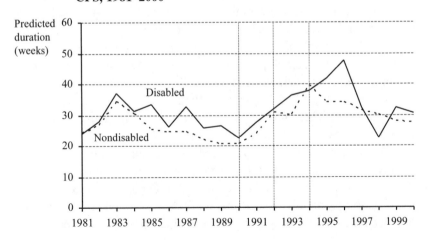

disabled worker with a particular job. This behavior would be consistent with a risk-averse employer who has more difficulty determining the productivity of disabled workers than of nondisabled workers from observable traits. This could be due to lack of experience on the part of the employer or because there is greater variance in the productivity among disabled workers for any given set of observable characteristics.

Effectiveness of Search Methods

One important quality that an individual brings to the job search is the type of strategies used. It is of interest to determine whether disabled job seekers consistently use different search strategies and whether those methods are consistently more or less effective for disabled searchers than for the nondisabled. Several researchers have found that certain search methods are more effective in finding employment than others (Bortnick and Ports 1992; Thomas 1991), so if disabled individuals are systematically relying on less effective methods, or systematically have less effective methods available, this leads to an obvious remedy. Figure 5.7 details the average percentage of disabled and nondisabled job seekers using each of six search strategies ("did nothing" is excluded as a strategy from the illustration).

Figure 5.7 Percentage of Disabled and Nondisabled Searchers Using Each Search Strategy, Averaged over the Period 1981–2000, CPS

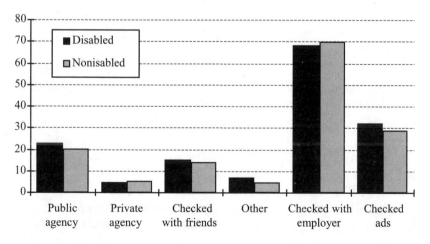

Disabled searchers are marginally more likely to check with friends, public agencies, and advertisements. None of the differences across strategies, however, is significantly different from zero. The implication, then, is that disabled and nondisabled job seekers rely, in the same percentages, on the same search strategies. In addition, there is no trend over time in the proportion of people using each method across disabled or nondisabled searchers.

Furthermore, out of the 100 possible coefficients (across years and across search strategies) included to control for potential differential impacts of search strategies on length of search for disabled workers, only 17 were significantly different from zero and not in any consistent way. In other words, each strategy never helped or hindered disabled searchers, relative to nondisabled searchers, in any systematic way. The implication is that personal demographics were the primary determinants of search outcome, and that merely changing strategies will not improve those outcomes for disabled workers.

CONCLUSIONS

The "not working" side of the labor market can be important in shaping the overall experience of a worker. This chapter compares the separation, unemployment, and job search experiences of disabled and nondisabled workers over time. The lower probability for disabled workers that a separation is involuntary is clearly good news for disabled workers. It implies that disabled individuals are not "marginal" workers, as some have theorized. The higher probability for this group that a separation is voluntary indicates, at a minimum, that disabled workers do enjoy some labor market mobility with which they can seek out the most accommodating employment setting. It may also show that disabled workers have a more difficult time finding a good employment match, which is not entirely unexpected, or that health conditions necessitate more frequent voluntary movements in and out of jobs. There is no indication from the analysis performed here that the ADA has had much impact on the probability that a disabled worker's separation is either voluntary or involuntary.

Disabled workers are more likely to be reentrants and new entrants into unemployment than nondisabled workers. This is unfortunate because leaving and reentering the labor market typically results in less advantageous outcomes than movements between jobs.[15] There are not a lot of policy options, sadly, that might alter this pattern, since much of the movement into and out of the labor market may be dictated by the nature of the disabled worker's mental or physical condition.

On average over the time period, an unemployed disabled worker searches three weeks longer than a similar nondisabled worker before locating a job. This result, in combination with the finding that disabled workers are less likely to separate from his/her job for involuntary reasons, suggests that employers are being more "careful" in their hiring of disabled workers. There is a fine line between discrimination and being discriminating. However, it was also found that differences in individual characteristics between disabled and nondisabled workers explain most of the difference in their search spell lengths. Therefore, it is possible that the characteristics of disabled and nondisabled workers are being valued equally (the typical measure for discrimination), but that employers go to greater lengths to discern the fit of a disabled worker's endowments with a particular job. This behavior on the part of the employer would result both in longer search spells for the disabled and in a lower probability that a separation is involuntary.

These results, taken together, suggest that policies that assist employers and disabled workers in finding each other would go a long way to improving search outcomes. Active job placement and objective screening of skills might be useful and serve the needs of the "discerning" employer.

Notes

1. While it may seem natural to first focus on the *incidence* of separation, the employment analysis contained in Chapter 2 essentially contains the inverse of an analysis of incidence. The CPS does not ask separation questions of those who are currently working, so that an evaluation of separation incidence would amount to an analysis of unemployment incidence (the inverse of what was evaluated in Chapter 2). The results from Chapter 2 indicate that the disabled are more likely at any given time to have separated from their job, and that the difference in probability across disability status is unchanged over time.
2. Unpublished data from the U.S. Bureau of Labor Statistics; obtained November 2001.
3. The sample for whom these statistics were plotted consisted of those who spent at least some (no matter how little) time working in the previous year. This gives

us a better picture of the looking-for-work activity of those with at least some marginal attachment to the labor market.

4. The data used to generate Figure 5.2 and details of the questionnaire change are found in Table C.9 in Appendix C.

5. Multinomial logits have come under frequent criticism because of the assumption of independence of irrelevant alternatives (IIA) that is implied by the logit specification. Alternative specifications that retain the desired probability structure (i.e., multinomial probit) are riddled with their own problems and not considered here to add value greater than the cost that would be imposed. It has been pointed out that under the framework of what is called a "universal" logit, the estimation procedure can be applied, but the utility interpretation of the structural estimates is lost. In addition, the more regressors included to describe the multiple outcomes, the less bothersome is the assumption of IIA. For these reasons, the logit structure is retained. For further discussion on these points, see Ben-Akiva and Lerman (1985, section 5.2) and Moffitt (1999, pp. 1382–1387).

6. Voluntary separations included the following reasons: personal, family, school; personal/family (includes pregnancy); return to school; health; retirement/old age; and unsatisfactory work arrangements (hours/pay/etc.). Involuntary separation included the following reasons: seasonal job completed, temporary seasonal or intermittent job completed, slack work/business, and temporary nonseasonal job completed. The analysis in this chapter is based only on those who experienced a separation either in the past five years (1981–1993) or in the previous year (1994–1999); the results, therefore, are not generalizable to the entire labor force.

7. The predicted probabilities are found in Table C.10 in Appendix C. Whereas the impact of the questionnaire change was obvious in the raw data (see Figure 5.2), the predicted probabilities are comparable across years in the cross section, with the primary impact being larger sample sizes prior to 1994.

8. U.S. Department of Labor, *Employment and Earnings* (January 2001, p. 203). To be counted as unemployed, the respondent must have undertaken some action within the past four weeks to find a job.

9. The predicted probabilities from the multinomial logit analysis used to generate these figures are found in Table C.11 in Appendix C. The figures plot a "smoothed" version of the series of numbers reported in Table C.11.

10. This simply involves calculating a least squares third-order polynomial fit through the data points.

11. Following the suggestion of Akerlof and Main (1981) to compensate for the deficiencies of the job search data collected by the CPS, expected search duration is calculated as twice the observed duration at a given point in time. This representation of expected duration relies on the assumption of a steady state, which may be difficult to support for a statistic across time (i.e., business cycles; Sider 1985); however, this may be less critical when making cross-sectional comparisons, as is done here. It is also assumed that this assumption has the same implication across disability status.

12. The numbers used to prepare Figure 5.5 can be found in Table C.12 (column 1) in Appendix C.

13. See note 11.
14. Predicted expected duration was calculated using the coefficient estimates resulting from the accelerated failure time model. Where search duration is assumed to be distributed as a Weibull, expected search duration is calculated as $E[t_i|t_i > 0;X_i,\beta,\sigma] = \exp(X_i'\beta)\Gamma(1 + \sigma)$, where Γ is the gamma distribution function. The characteristics (other than disability) for which the predicted expected durations were calculated (X) are the means corresponding to the entire sample. See Long (1997). The numbers used to prepare Figure 5.6 can be found in Table C.12 (columns 2 and 3) in Appendix C.
15. There is even some evidence that disabled workers experience more discrimination *between* employers (from switching jobs) than they experience with any given employer (on their current job). See O'Hara (2000). The implication is that any job separation may worsen a disabled person's labor market outcome.

6
State versus Federal Legislation

Whenever major federal legislation to regulate the functioning of a market is enacted, a key question raised is whether that law is redundant or whether it has the potential of actually altering the functioning of the market (i.e., is "binding"). By the time the ADA was passed, all states had some form of legislation addressing discrimination against the disabled (see Table 6.1).[1] Thus, the environment in which the ADA was approved was arguably already a post-ADA one. One might suggest that the ADA was superfluous; the states were already addressing the problem of discrimination against the disabled and there was no need for federal legislation. This situation may be an explanation for finding no or very little labor market impact attributable to the ADA in previous chapters. In other words, it may be the case that the state legislation "crowded out" any potential impact of the ADA. On the other hand, legislation at the state level may have served as a statement of ethical beliefs already integrated into the economy.

To determine whether state-level protective legislation "crowded out" or had a differential impact on the experience of disabled workers than the federal ADA, employment, wage, and hours analyses mirroring those contained in Chapters 2, 3, and 4 are repeated here, but only for a subsample of states that enacted disability legislation between 1981 (the beginning of available data) and 1991 (the last year before implementation of the federal legislation). The employment impact is determined by estimation of a pooled, cross-sectional bivariate probit with selection model analogous to that estimated in Chapter 2. The state-level impact of disability legislation on wages is determined by a pooled, cross-sectional estimation of log wages, controlling for selection into the labor market, mirroring the wage analysis in Chapter 3. The bivariate probit with selection will again be used to parallel the part-time employment analysis of Chapter 4. Only the CPS data set will be used for analyses in this chapter.

The condition for being included in the subsample for analysis is whether the worker resided in a state that adopted protection for the disabled during this period.[2] To coincide with the provisions of the

Table 6.1 Summary of State-Level Disability Legislation

State	First year disability legislation in place	Public/private coverage	State	First year disability legislation in place	Public/private coverage
Alabama	1975	public	Montana	1974	public/private
Alaska	1987	public/private[a]	Nebraska	1971	public
Arizona	1985	public/private	Nevada	1973	public/private
Arkansas	1973	public	New Hampshire	1971	public/private
California	1993	public/private	New Jersey	1975	public/private
Colorado	1980	public/private[a]	New Mexico	1978	public/private
Connecticut	1979	public/private	New York	1973	public/private
Delaware	1973	public/private	North Carolina	1974	public/private[a]
Florida	Before 1988	public	North Dakota	1985	public/private
Georgia	1988	public/private	Ohio	1983	public/private
Hawaii	1977	public/private	Oklahoma	1976	public/private[a]
Idaho	1978	public	Oregon	1981	public/private
Illinois	1981	public/private	Pennsylvania	1973	public/private
Indiana	1981	public/private	Rhode Island	1974	public/private

State	Year	Coverage
Idaho	1969	public
Illinois	1988	public/private
Indiana	1980	public/private
Iowa	1975	public/private
	Before 1971	public
Kansas	1972	public/private[a]
Kentucky	1974	public/private
Louisiana	1976	public/private
	1975	public
	1980	public/private
Maine	1973	public/private[a]
Maryland	1974	public/private
Massachusetts	1983	public/private
Michigan	1976	public/private
Minnesota	1973	public/private
Mississippi	1974	public
Missouri	1978	public/private
Rhode Island	1973	public/private
South Carolina	1972	public
	1996	public/private
South Dakota	1973	public
	1984	public/private[a]
Tennessee	1976	public/private
Texas	1989	public/private
Utah	1979	public/private
Vermont	1981	public/private
Virginia	1972	public
Washington	1973	public/private[a]
Washington, DC	Before 1972	public
	1994	public/private
West Virginia	1981	public/private
Wisconsin	1965	public/private
Wyoming	1985	public/private[a]

NOTE: Some further details of each of these state's laws can be found in Appendix D.
[a] Exact original coverage not available; classification based on current coverage definitions.

ADA, the date at which legislation covering both public and private employers became effective was used to distinguish pre- and post-time periods. As can be seen from Table 6.1, 10 states passed disability legislation between (but not including) 1981 and 1991. These states were Alaska (1987), Arizona (1985), Delaware (1988), Idaho (1988), Massachusetts (1988), North Carolina (1985), North Dakota (1983), South Dakota (1984), Texas (1989), and Wyoming (1985).

A preliminary look at the potential impact on employment probabilities and labor force participation is shown in Figures 6.1 and 6.2, which plot these statistics for the disabled and the nondisabled. These

Figure 6.1 Labor Force Participation Rates for the Disabled and the Nondisabled, CPS, 1981–1991

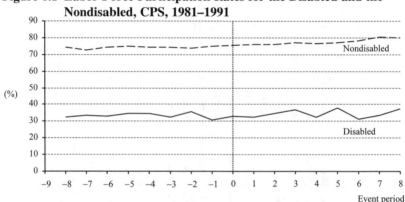

Figure 6.2 Proportion of Disabled and Nondisabled Labor Force Participants That Are Employed, CPS, 1981–1991

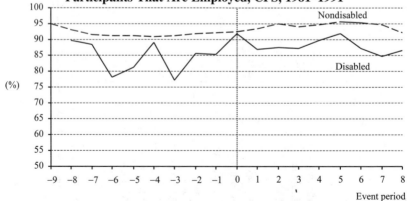

illustrations show the averages across all 10 states, event-study style, with $t = 0$ corresponding to the year disability legislation was in place in the state; $t < 0$ corresponds to the pre-legislation period and $t \geq 0$ corresponds to the post-legislation period. There is no obvious change in either the labor force participation rate or conditional employment rate for either the disabled or nondisabled, except for perhaps a higher employment rate for both groups, in the post-legislation period.

IMPACT ON EMPLOYMENT

To determine the employment impact of state-level disability legislation, a pooled, cross-sectional bivariate probit model with selection was estimated with dummy variables representing whether the observation shows up in the data pre-legislation or post-legislation and whether the observation is a disabled or nondisabled person. These dummy variables were also interacted to determine whether being disabled had any greater effect on employment after the legislation than before, relative to the experience of a nondisabled person.[3] The bivariate specification allows for the two outcomes (labor force participation and employment) to be impacted by the same unobservable factors (e.g., motivation). The selectivity part of the model is merely a recognition that we do not get to see the employment outcome unless the person is in the labor market to begin with, and that those we observe in the labor market may have systematically different employment outcomes than those not in the labor market. Correcting for selectivity allows us to make inferences for anyone from the population, not just those we observe in the labor market; this is what makes the probability unconditional.

The empirical model is specified as follows:

$$(6.1) \quad \text{LFP}_{is} = \alpha_1 + \gamma_1' X_{1i} + \beta_1 \text{DISABLE}_i + \phi_1 \text{POST}_s$$
$$+ \theta_1 \text{ DISABLE}_i \times \text{POST}_s + \epsilon_{1is}$$
$$\text{EMP}_{is} = \alpha_2 + \gamma_2' X_{2i} + \beta_2 \text{DISABLE}_i + \phi_2 \text{POST}_s$$
$$+ \theta_2 \text{ DISABLE}_i \times \text{POST}_s + \epsilon_{2is}$$

$\text{EMP}_{is} = 1$ if person i in state s is employed, 0 otherwise; $\text{LFP}_{is} = 1$ if person i in state s is in the labor force, 0 otherwise, and EMP_{is} is not observed unless $LFP_{is} = 1$. $DISABLE_i$ is equal to 1 if person i is disabled, 0 otherwise; X_{1i} and X_{2i} include individual demographic characteristics; $POST_s$ is equal to 1 if person is observed in state s post legislation for that state; ϵ_{1is} and ϵ_{2is} are distributed as a bivariate normal with means equal to 0, variances equal to 1, and correlation equal to ρ; and α_j, γ_j, β_j, φ_j, and θ_j $(j = 1,2)$ are parameters to be estimated.

In this framework, the affected group (the disabled) is controlled for by a dummy variable indicating whether the individual has a work-limiting disability, and the time period is controlled for by a dummy variable indicating whether disability legislation in the state had been implemented yet or not. Given the nonlinearity of the bivariate probit estimation procedure, a single parameter coefficient does not tell us the additional effect the legislation had on the difference in employment probabilities between the disabled and nondisabled; however, the significance of the coefficient on the interacted $DISABLE_i \times POST_s$ will yield significance levels of that impact. Table 6.2 details the results from the estimation.

The first thing to notice from Table 6.2 is that the parameter estimates on the vast majority of regressors are of the same sign and the same magnitude as those in Table 2.1 in Chapter 2, corresponding to the national sample. The only exceptions to this are the west, central city, college, and advanced degree dummy variables; and the state unemployment rate (the signs across the tables are the same, but the magnitudes differ slightly) and the Midwest dummy variable (less significant in the state analysis). The implication of the similarity across the national and state-level analyses is that the observations in this subset of states are not at all far from the norm and that the results on the regressors of interest (those related to disability status) should be considered generalizable beyond these states.

The second result to note from Table 6.2 is the lack of significance of the coefficient on the $DISABLE \times POST$ regressor in the employment equation. This means that the employment probability of a disabled person, relative to a nondisabled person, did not change post-legislation. Again, in a set of results where most other regressors are significant at the 99 percent confidence level, this is notable.

The lack of impact of the ADA at the national level could have been the result of state legislation crowding out any potential effect of the federal law, in which case we should see an influence of enactment

Table 6.2 Labor Force Participation and Employment Bivariate Probit with Selection Results, CPS, 1981–1991

Regressor	Labor force participation equation	Employment equation
Intercept	−2.9613***	0.8355***
	(0.0492)	(0.2396)
Age (00)	13.3187***	−1.2545***
	(0.2278)	(0.3533)
Age Squared (0000)	−16.4768***	2.3317***
	(0.2828)	(0.4673)
Female = 1	−0.5123***	0.2041
	(0.010)	(0.0143)
Nonwhite = 1	−0.0340**	−0.2871***
	(0.0148)	(0.0194)
High school grad = 1	0.2689***	0.0614***
	(0.0127)	(0.0180)
Some college = 1	0.1187***	0.1680***
	(0.0135)	(0.0198)
College grad = 1	0.3347***	0.3606***
	(0.1784)	(0.0262)
Advanced degree = 1	0.1836***	0.1843***
	(0.0310)	(0.0463)
Central city = 1	0.0781***	−0.0040
	(0.0150)	(0.0216)
Midwest = 1	−0.0406**	0.0010
	(0.0175)	(0.0336)
South = 1	0.0108	0.0771***
	(0.0142)	(0.0222)
West = 1	−0.1120***	0.0788***
	(0.0166)	(0.0298)
Single household = 1	0.2345***	—
	(0.0117)	
Nonlabor income (000000)	−21.2445***	—
	(0.8830)	
Worked last year = 1	1.9908***	—
	(0.0110)	
Weeks worked last year (00)	—	3.0181***
		(0.0457)
State unemployment rate (0)	−0.0389	−0.8264***
	(0.0334)	(0.0483)

Table 6.2 (continued)

Regressor	Labor force participation equation	Employment equation
Real gross state product (000000)	—	0.0593
		(0.1539)
Log population	—	−0.0042
		(0.0159)
DISABLE = 1	−0.7197***	−0.2095***
	(0.0301)	(0.0514)
POST legislation = 1	0.0442***	−0.0273
	(0.0127)	(0.0185)
DISABLE × POST = 1	−0.0523	0.0057
	(0.0377)	(0.0663)
Rho		0.0403***
		(0.0065)
Log-likelihood		−65,190
Number of observations		140,707

NOTE: States included in the analysis are Alaska, Arizona, Delaware, Idaho, Massachusetts, North Carolina, North Dakota, South Dakota, Texas, and Wyoming.
Standard errors are in parentheses.
*** = significant at the 99 percent confidence level.
** = significant at the 95 percent confidence level.
Notation of, for example (00), indicates regressor has been scaled by dividing by 100.

of disability legislation at the state level. Alternatively, it may be the case, as has been pointed out with other social legislation, that the law itself merely was the culmination of changes already incorporated into the labor market experience of the affected group. In this instance, we should see no effect of enactment of such legislation at the state level either. This latter scenario is what we observe. While, overall, persons with disabilities have a lower probability of unconditional employment, there is no relative change in that employment probability post-legislation versus pre-legislation.

The third result of particular interest is related to the determination of labor force participation. Recall that in the national analysis (see Table 2.1) there was a dramatic decline in labor force participation rates among the disabled post-ADA. If, indeed, the ADA legislation caused individuals to flee the labor market, similar legislation at the state level should result in the same behavior. The results in Table 6.2, however, indicate that state-level disability legislation had no such impact; the coefficient on DISABLE × POST in the labor force participation equation is not significantly different from zero. Again, this is in an estimation where nearly all the other regressors are significant at the 99 percent confidence level. These findings support the theory posited in Chapter 2 that the drop in the labor force participation rate that occurred in 1994 at the national level (see Figure 2.2) cannot be attributable to the ADA and is likely the result of some other confounding factor (i.e., modifications in welfare and Social Security Administration policies).

Lastly, while the state unemployment rate has a large negative impact on employment probabilities, the new regressors of real gross state product and log population are insignificant determinants of employment; the positive sign of real gross state product does, however, make intuitive sense.

IMPACT ON WAGES

It was found in Chapter 3 that the ADA seems to have had a negative impact on wages of disabled workers overall, although it did not appear to be directly related to the cost of accommodations required of firms covered by the legislation. This section looks at the state level to see whether a similar impact on wages occurred when protective legislation was passed.

Log real wages are specified as a function of demographic and job characteristics, as well as indicators for disability status, time period, and the interaction between disability status and time. The following specification is estimated via OLS for the time period 1981–1991:

$$(6.2) \quad \text{LNRWAGE}_{is} = \alpha + \gamma X_i + \beta_1 \text{DISABLE}_i + \beta_2 \text{POST}_s + \beta_3 \text{DISABLE}_i \times \text{POST}_s + \epsilon_{is}$$

where LNRWAGE_{is} is the natural log hourly real (1982–1984 = 1) wage of worker i in state s,

X_i is a set of covariates for each person (demographic and job characteristics),

DISABLE_i is equal to 1 if person i has a work-limiting disability, and

POST_s is equal to 1 if person is observed in state s post-legislation for that state.

The affected group (the disabled) is controlled for by a dummy variable indicating whether the individual has a work-limiting disability, and the post-legislation time period in each state is controlled for by a dummy variable indicating whether disability legislation was in place yet or not. The coefficient of interest (β_3) measures the change in real wages, relative to nondisabled workers, after passage of disability legislation, relative to before legislation was in place. X_i includes individual demographic and job characteristics.

Wages are observed for workers only, and because the characteristics of workers may be changing over time in unobservable ways, it is important to control for any potential unobserved self-selection into the labor market. Consequently, Equation 6.2 is modified by simply adding the standard inverse-Mills ratio obtained from the first-stage probit estimation of a labor force participation/employment equation. This standard Heckman (1979) two-step procedure for controlling for self-selection is presented in greater detail in Chapter 3. The parameters of the model are identified through some regressors in the first-stage probit estimation that are not in the wage regression; these regressors include nonlabor income and an indicator of whether the person worked last year or not. Since the purpose of this two-stage approach is merely to obtain unbiased estimates of the coefficients in the wage equation, interpretation of those coefficients is not changed by controlling for selection. Table 6.3 contains the estimation results from the log wage equation estimation.

As with the employment analysis, the results in Table 6.3 mirror those at the national level, as reported in Table 3.1 in Chapter 3; most coefficients on the control variables are of the same sign, and they are roughly of the same magnitude. Two exceptions are the coefficient on the advanced degree dummy variable, which is about one third the size of that estimated at the national level, and the coefficient on the selection term. In Chapter 3, there was evidence of positive self-selection, meaning that those entering the labor market could expect to earn higher wages than the population as a whole. In the state-level analysis, the coefficient on the selection term is negative, indicating that those entering the labor market typically will earn less than the population as a whole. Since the purpose of controlling for selection is to obtain consistent estimates of the other coefficients in the wage equation, this difference in sign between the national and state-level analy-

Table 6.3 Log Real Wage OLS Estimation with Selection, CPS, 1981–1991

Regressor	Labor force participation equation
Intercept	2.5415***
	(0.0509)
Age (00)	0.0415***
	(0.0051)
Age Squared (0000)	−0.0004
	(0.0140)
Female = 1	−0.2266***
	(0.0048)
Nonwhite = 1	−0.0416***
	(0.0042)
High school grad = 1	0.1230***
	(0.0046)
Some college = 1	0.2072***
	(0.0055)
College grad = 1	0.3863***
	(0.0067)
Advanced degree = 1	0.1071***
	(0.0032)
Midwest = 1	−0.3072***
	(0.0010)
South = 1	−0.1441***
	(0.0000)
West = 1	−0.1125***
	(0.0001)
Hours worked per week	0.0017
	(0.0142)
Union = 1	0.1496***
	(0.0008)
Single household = 1	−0.0659***
	(0.0033)
State unemployment rate (0)	0.0109***
	(0.0003)
Real gross state product (000000)	0.0081
	(0.0052)
Log population	−0.0953***
	(0.0047)
DISABLE = 1	−0.0802***
	(0.0033)

Table 6.3 (continued)

Regressor	Labor force participation equation
POST legislation = 1	0.0307***
	(0.0039)
DISABLE × POST = 1	−0.0452**
	(0.0176)
λ (selection term)	−0.0811***
	(0.0057)
R^2	0.46
F statistic	2,354
Number of observations	95,604

NOTE: States included in the analysis are Alaska, Arizona, Delaware, Idaho, Massachusetts, North Carolina, North Dakota, South Dakota, Texas, and Wyoming. The wage regression also included seven industry and five occupational dummy variables, and a government dummy variable not reported here. The first-stage probit estimation included age; age squared; gender, race, education, and disability dummies; and the state unemployment rate. Nonlabor income and an indicator of working last year were included as identifying regressors. All estimated coefficients in the first-stage estimation were significantly different from zero at the 99 percent confidence level. Standard errors are in parentheses.
*** = significant at the 99 percent confidence level.
** = significant at the 95 percent confidence level.

ses is not a concern here but may be worth exploring elsewhere from a behavioral perspective.

The coefficient on the interaction term (DISABLE × POST) is −0.0452, indicating that disabled workers experienced a 4.5 percent decline in wages, relative to nondisabled workers, post-disability legislation, relative to pre-disability legislation. This is roughly of the same magnitude as the 3 percent decline in wages experienced post-ADA implementation (see Table 3.1). The implication is that we see the same relative decline in wages of disabled versus nondisabled persons at the state and national levels. This may mean that the measured impact of the federal ADA on relative wages is muted, given that some adjustment to disability legislation had already taken place as a result of state laws. In addition, this lower wage of disabled workers relative to that of nondisabled workers may not be the consequence of adjustment cost, but, rather, reflect the overall negative impact on the disabled, not just those covered by the legislation; this was the result discovered in Chapter 3.

IMPACT ON HOURS

The increase in part-time employment post-ADA found in Chapter 4 is worth exploring at the state level, as well. It is of interest since flexibility in hours may serve as an important mechanism through which employers can accommodate many types of disabilities. If this is the case, then requirements to accommodate workers' disabilities at the state level should result in similar adjustments as seen post-ADA. Figure 6.3 plots the average proportion across states of disabled and nondisabled workers that are employed part-time. The reference vertical line corresponds to the time when legislation was in place in each state. There appears to be an increase in the proportion of disabled workers that are employed part-time, as well as a modest divergence in the two series.

The pooled, cross-sectional analysis of Chapter 4 is repeated here in order to determine whether there is any significant growth in part-time employment among disabled workers, post-legislation, relative to

Figure 6.3 Proportion of Disabled and Nondisabled Workers That Are Employed Part-Time, CPS, 1981–1991

nondisabled workers. The model estimated is the bivariate probit with selection:

$$
\begin{aligned}
\text{(6.3)} \quad \text{EMP}_{is} &= \alpha_1 + \gamma_1' X_{1i} + \beta_1 \, \text{DISABLE}_i + \phi_1 \, \text{POST}_s \\
&\quad + \theta_1 \, \text{DISABLE}_i \times \text{POST}_s + \epsilon_{1is} \\
\text{PT}_{is} &= \alpha_2 + \gamma_2' X_{2i} + \beta_2 \, \text{DISABLE}_i + \phi_2 \, \text{POST}_s \\
&\quad + \theta_2 \, \text{DISABLE}_i \times \text{POST}_s + \epsilon_{2is}.
\end{aligned}
$$

$\text{EMP}_{is} = 1$ if person i in state s is employed, 0 otherwise, and $\text{PT}_{is} = 1$ if person i in state s is employed part-time and is not observed unless $\text{EMP}_{is} = 1$. DISABLE_i is equal to 1 if person i is disabled, 0 otherwise; POST_s is equal to 1 if the person is observed after passage of the state legislation; X_{1i} and X_{2i} include individual demographic characteristics; ϵ_{1is} and ϵ_{2is} are distributed as a bivariate normal with means equal to 0, variances equal to 1, and correlation equal to ρ.

Again, the coefficient in the part-time equation on the DISABLE $\times$ POST regressor is what tells us whether there is any change in the probability of part-time employment among disabled workers, post-legislation, relative to nondisabled workers. Table 6.4 details the regression results. Using the parameter estimates, the difference in the impact of having a work-limiting disability on part-time employment across the two time periods can be calculated by evaluating the probabilities of interest for each person, varying the DISABLE and POST dummy variables, then taking the difference between these probabilities and averaging the differences across the sample. This calculation translates the estimated coefficients into a 2-percentage-point greater probability of disabled workers being employed part-time than nondisabled workers, post-legislation relative to pre-legislation. This result is only significantly different from zero at the 85 percent confidence level, but it does provide some support for the notion that disability legislation, whether by the states or national, influences the hours of work of disabled workers.[4] Also, as with the preceding wage analysis, these findings suggest that the impact of the ADA was dampened somewhat by the adjustments in hours that had already taken place as a result of the state-level legislation.

CONCLUSIONS

The goal of this chapter was to determine what impact state-level disability legislation has had on the employment, wage, and hours out-

**Table 6.4 Employment and Part-Time Employment Bivariate Probit
with Selection Results, CPS, 1981–1991**

Regressor	Employment equation	Part-time employment equation
DISABLE = 1	−0.1311***	0.3406***
	(0.0498)	(0.0462)
POST legislation = 1	−0.0280*	0.0208*
	(0.0165)	(0.0118)
DISABLE × POST = 1	0.0129	0.0828^
	(0.0654)	(0.0582)
Rho	0.7707***	
	(0.0169)	
Log-likelihood	−54,402	
Number of observations	101,584	

NOTE: States included in the analysis are Alaska, Arizona, Delaware, Idaho, Massa-chusetts, North Carolina, North Dakota, South Dakota, Texas, and Wyoming. Re-gressors included both in the employment and part-time employment equations (but not reported here) include age, education, region, race, gender, marital status, and central city residence indicator. Regressors unique to the employment equation in-clude the state unemployment rate and the number of weeks worked last year. Re-gressors unique to the part-time employment equation include occupation and industry dummies, nonlabor income, and a government employer indicator. Standard errors are in parentheses.
*** = significant at the 99 percent confidence level.
* = significant at the 90 percent confidence level.
^ = significant at the 85 percent confidence level.

comes of disabled workers. The question is whether the ADA is redun-dant with laws passed at the state level. The results indicate that the state-level legislation operates on the labor market in the same way as does the federal ADA. Namely, relative employment probabilities of persons with disabilities are not affected by state-level disability legis-lation. It was also found that labor force participation rates were unaf-fected by the state-level legislation, lending support for the theory that the decline in labor force participation rates observed post-ADA at the national level was not ADA-induced. In addition, the disabled also experienced a relative wage decline and a tentative rise in relative part-time employment at the state level following legislation.

The main implication of these results is that the lack of impact of the ADA on employment, while perhaps disappointing to proponents, is consistent with the contention that this type of legislation arrives after society has already adopted its main principles, both at the national and the state level. On the other hand, observing similar wage and hours effects in states and nationally indicates that the wage and hours impacts of the ADA would likely have been greater in magnitude had the disabled not already partially experienced the impact of protective legislation at the state level. The analyses in this chapter clearly indicate that state-level disability legislation did not fully crowd out the impact of the ADA (not at all regarding employment, and potentially only partially regarding wages and hours). Can we conclude, then, that the ADA was redundant? The answer is "no." There was no employment effect to crowd out (no employment effect at the national level), and there was still a measurable impact on wages and hours at the national level. In addition, the federal legislation served as a mechanism to instill uniformity of expectations of employers (even though some state laws have a broader definition of coverage), and it brought the issue of discrimination against disabled workers to the national forefront.

Notes

1. Also see Advisory Commission on Intergovernmental Relations (1989) for additional information.
2. Methodologies that take advantage of differing legislative statuses among states (or, more generally, across observations) have often been referred to as "natural experiments" and have been applied by a number of researchers. For example, see Chay (1996) and Carrington, McCue, and Pierce (2000).
3. The strategy described here can be likened to a differences-in-differences (DD) methodology but is applied to a nonlinear statistical model. While this type of pooled, cross-sectional analysis has been used by many researchers (for example, Card 1992; Gruber 1994 and 1996; Zveglich and Rodgers 1996; and Hamermesh and Trejo 2000), the technique also has its critics (such as Heckman 1996). The primary criticism of this approach is that it is impossible to control for unobserved changes in the environment that occurred at the same time as the event of interest. The concern is mitigated in the analysis in this chapter, however, by the fact that the post-legislation period varies across states.
4. Also, similar to the approach in Chapter 4, an additional analysis was performed to determine whether, as at the national level, there was a marked increase in voluntary part-time employment, but the results were inconclusive. The coefficient on the interaction DISABLE $\times$ POST term was not significantly different from zero, and the adjusted R^2 was only 0.08.

7
Conclusions and Policy Implications

This book has examined and documented the relative labor market experience of workers with disabilities with an eye to evaluating the impact of the ADA. A worker's labor market experience goes beyond simply whether a person has a job and what he or she is being paid. While these dimensions are fundamental, the quality or characteristics of the worker's job, the process of obtaining it, and the nature of job separation are also important factors. One intention of the ADA is to break down *barriers in* the labor market; thus the focus of all analyses in this book is on the experience of the disabled in that environment, not on factors that influence decisions to enter the labor market. Accounting for those choices, however, is important in obtaining results generalizable to the disabled population, so measures are taken, where appropriate, to control for the decision to seek employment. In addition to the multiple dimensions of the potential impact of the ADA on disabled Americans in the labor market, there are at least as many more ways in which the ADA affects the lives of all disabled Americans; such issues are not the subject of this work, but they may in fact amount to a much greater overall effect than that experienced by disabled workers alone.

Overall, the analyses presented here lead to the conclusion that the labor market experience of disabled workers is quantitatively lower in all dimensions than that of nondisabled workers. In addition, while this relative situation has improved over time in some ways, there is no strong evidence that it has been substantively impacted by the ADA. There are two primary reasons why the ADA may not have had the hoped-for dramatic effect. It could be the case that no one is paying attention to the legislation. In other words, employers may not be complying (either through lack of awareness or refusal) with the mandates of the ADA, workers may not be aware of their rights under the law, or workers may not be pursuing these rights. Alternatively, it may be the case that the bulk of the experience of disabled workers in the labor market is being defined by factors other than those corrected for by the ADA.

It is not likely that the former is the case. For example, cognizance of the ADA is widespread. A 1999 Harris poll indicated that 67 percent of those surveyed were aware of the ADA, and it is likely that even a higher percentage of people with disabilities (and employers) know of the legislation (Roper Center for Public Opinion Research 1999). In addition, the rate of ADA litigation suggests that disabled workers are actively pursuing their rights. After climbing to a height of almost 20,000 in 1995, the number of claims tapered off to about 16,000 in 2001.[1] Lastly, there is evidence that at least large employers and municipalities are complying with the provisions of the ADA (see Scheid 1998; Condrey and Brudney 1998). Additional evidence of compliance is implied by the Equal Employment Opportunity Commission's "determination of no reasonable cause to believe that discrimination occurred based upon evidence obtained in investigation" in 54.1 percent (fiscal year 2001) of the ADA charges made.[2] This statistic has stayed at 54 percent or higher since 1996.

It is probable, therefore, that the lack of notable impact of the ADA on the labor market experience of the disabled implies that, like many other pieces of legislation with a strong social and moral content, it was adopted in an environment that had already embraced its principles and mandates, for the most part. For example, by 1990, every state had adopted some form of legislation granting protection to disabled workers. Results in Chapter 6 indicate that these state-level policies had influences on employment, wages, and hours similar to those found when the federal legislation was implemented. The implication is that some of the anticipated effect of the ADA had already been experienced at the state level over a longer period of time, beginning typically in the 1970s. This is not to say that the ADA was an unnecessary piece of legislation from the perspective of the labor market. Even if the ADA merely reflects the environment in which it was passed, it serves to strongly proclaim our social values and to provide a uniform legal mechanism with which to arrest the activities of those who have not yet embraced those values. As such, however, we are left with the nagging question of, "What do we do now to improve the labor market experience of workers with disabilities?" The results of the analyses presented in this book can provide some guidance in answering this question.

The dimensions of a worker's labor market experience evaluated include employment, compensation, hours of work, distribution across and representation in occupations and industries, job separation, unemployment, and job search. The CPS is the primary source of data for each analysis. Various repeated cross-sectional and pooled cross-sectional analyses were performed with data spanning the years 1981–2000. Some of the analyses were supplemented with information in the SIPP. The SIPP is primarily used to identify whether any experience or impact differs across *type* of disability. The years of analyses with the SIPP are limited to 1986–1997 but generally confirm the conclusions from the longer data series available from the CPS. The results of most notable interest are summarized in the following discussion and are accompanied by policy recommendations. This chapter ends with an overall assessment of the implications of the findings for the ADA and beyond.

EMPLOYMENT INCENTIVES

Chapter 2 presents evidence that while the joint labor force participation and employment outcome declined among the disabled (driven by a decreasing labor force participation rate), the unconditional employment probability of the disabled did not change, relative to that of the nondisabled. In other words, the employment prospects for the disabled, while not improved by the ADA, were also not harmed. Analysis of the SIPP data set revealed that workers with mental disabilities (and disabilities classified as "other") actually experienced an *increase* in employment relative to the nondisabled. This may be the result of easier accommodation of mental impairments or the recent emphasis on providing employment opportunities for the mentally disabled by the Presidential Task Force on Employment of Adults with Disabilities (formerly, the President's Committee on Employment of People with Disabilities).[3] In addition, there has been a relative gain in employment in large firms among the disabled, as compared with the nondisabled; of course, large employers are those most able to absorb the cost of accommodation. These results lead to some obvious policy suggestions: providing incentives for the disabled to enter the labor force and facilitating the accommodation process.

Incentives for the Disabled

The most recent initiative to encourage labor force participation among the disabled is the Ticket to Work and Work Incentives Improvement Act of 1999; it applies to recipients of Supplemental Security Income (SSI) or Social Security Disability Insurance (SSDI) government cash payment programs for people with disabilities. The main provisions that encourage labor force participation under these programs involve reducing the risk and cost associated with "trying" work. One provision is a disregard for impairment-related work expenses (e.g., special equipment modified to accommodate a worker's disability, medical devices, and special transportation needs). These expenses are deducted from a worker's income before it is evaluated for payment eligibility purposes. In order to encourage and facilitate labor force participation, this provision could be expanded to provide for direct reimbursement of these fixed (out-of-pocket) expenses. The criteria for determining reimbursement could be the same for current deductibility.

Another current work incentive provision allows for the exclusion of earned income for SSI recipients. Under this policy, the first $65 a month and half of the remainder of earnings are disregarded in calculating the SSI payment amount. This provision could be made more generous and match that of the Trial Work Period (TWP) available for SSDI recipients. The TWP allows SSDI recipients to work for nine months without any reduction in benefit payments; after that period, payments are discontinued if the person is able to maintain his or her work activity.

The continuation of Medicare and Medicaid benefits beyond SSI or SSDI eligibility is an important feature of the current incentives. Many jobs for which disabled workers can qualify might not offer benefits, especially if the person must work part-time in order to accommodate his or her impairment. In addition, the extended period of eligibility (SSDI) and reinstatement of payments without a new application (SSI) are important safety nets for the disabled worker not sure if he or she should give employment a try. These provisions basically allow recipients to reinstate payments without once again going through the lengthy application process if they discover they are not yet ready to permanently enter or reenter the labor force. SSDI can be reinstated up to 36 months after ineligibility, but former SSI recipients only have 12 months to apply for reinstatement. While the SSI time allowance is considerably shorter than the SSDI time allowance, eligibility requirements for the programs likely necessitate this differentiation.

In addition to these programmatic incentives, strategies encouraging labor force participation among *all* disabled individuals (not just those receiving disability benefits) are warranted, based on the results in Chapter 2. One suggestion, the Disabled Worker Tax Credit (Burkhauser, Glenn, and Wittenburg 1997), would provide incentives similar to the current Earned Income Tax Credit for the working poor, but be targeted at the disabled worker. Under this program, disabled workers would essentially receive a subsidy to their employment wage. It is not clear whether this program, however, would be effective in improving the labor market experience along compensation or job quality dimensions. The subsidy may encourage disabled workers to take lower-paying jobs while not holding employers responsible for valuing the skills (with accommodation) of this group equally with those of non-disabled workers.

Incentives for Employers

There has been a shift of employment among disabled workers toward larger firms. The implication is that cost might be an important factor in the willingness to hire a person with disabilities, and if that cost were reduced, disabled labor force participants would make even greater gains in employment. The federal government currently provides tax incentives to smaller firms to help pay for the expense of accommodating workers with disabilities. Section 44 (Title 26) of the Internal Revenue Service (IRS) Code allows for a tax credit to cover 50 percent (up to $5,000) of an "eligible access expenditure" in one year incurred by a business with total revenues of $1 million or less, or 30 or fewer full-time employees (Hays 1999). Qualifying expenditures under this section include adaptations of existing structures and purchase of special equipment and services (such as sign language interpreters).[4] While this provision allows firms to be reimbursed for out-of-pocket expenses for accommodating disabled workers, the actual physical process of accommodating (i.e., evaluation of need and modification of the environment) distracts the organization from its primary focus of business. One thing the government could do to ease this situation would be to equip the disabled worker with knowledge and information regarding any specific accommodation he or she might require in the type of job being sought. It is not the intention of the ADA to put the burden of acquiring this background on the worker. However, the more information workers can provide and the easier they can make it for the employer, the better chance the individuals will not be seen merely for the burden they might cause, but for the attributes they provide to the firm.

The Work Opportunity Tax Credit (Title 26, Section 51 of the IRS Code) provides a tax credit for hiring individuals from specific target groups, with SSI recipients being one of those groups. The employer can claim 40 percent (up to $6,000) of the hired worker's first-year wages. The maximum credit applies to individuals employed at least 400 hours during the year, and lesser credit applies to those employed between 125 and 400 hours per year. While it is difficult to find the number of employers who have taken advantage of the tax credit opportunities associated with hiring the disabled, it is likely that these programs might suffer the same sort of administrative burdens that have resulted in the ineffectiveness of other tax credit and employment subsidy programs (for example, see Tannenwald 1982 and Katz 1998).

The Job Accommodations Network (JAN), sponsored by the Office of Disability Employment Policy of the U.S. Department of Labor, is a government resource that provides both employers and workers with valuable information. Network members share experiences in successful accommodation strategies; employers who utilize the service are required to join the network (Magill 1997).[5] One benefit provided by JAN is Searchable Online Accommodation Resource (SOAR), which allows someone on the Internet to go through a series of steps (select a disability, functional limitation, an affected job function, and an accommodation solution) and to obtain a list of vendors (from across the nation) providing the accommodation solution identified that could help a worker with a specified job function. There is also the opportunity on the SOAR website to enter specifics about an employer's or worker's unique situation and to obtain personal feedback. In addition, JAN provides information services to individuals with disabilities regarding starting a small business or becoming self-employed.

Armed with the data obtained through JAN, the disabled job seeker leaves the employer little excuse for not considering only the qualifications of the disabled applicant (i.e., productivity with accommodations in place). Clearly, if one could document the usefulness and success of these information dissemination efforts, a case might be made for devoting even more resources toward such efforts and perhaps providing regional consultants that could evaluate a worker's or employer's situation in person.

EDUCATION, TRAINING, AND JOB CHARACTERISTICS

One analysis in Chapter 3 indicates that the disabled overall have suffered a cost in terms of lower relative wages post-ADA. With the exception of large firms, wages of disabled workers declined by about 3 percent post-ADA, relative to those of nondisabled workers. People with musculoskeletal disabilities suffered the bulk of the wage loss. Policy suggestions made in the previous section to facilitate worker accommodation should also go toward improving the apparent compensation tax on disabled workers for whatever workplace adjustments are required. Further analysis in Chapter 3 indicates that these wage losses may not be directly related to accommodation costs, however, but are suffered by disabled workers whether or not they are covered by the ADA. By facilitating the accommodation process (through information and resources provided by JAN or some other organization), a person with disabilities is in a better position to negotiate a wage comparable to that of nondisabled individuals.

Decomposing the wage differential between disabled and nondisabled workers indicates that only about 30–40 percent of the gap is explained by observed characteristics of the workers themselves. While the remainder cannot all be interpreted as discrimination against the disabled, there is a significant portion of the differential that remains unexplained. Within the explained part, the greatest contributions to the wage discrepancy are made by differences in industry, occupation, and educational attainment. In addition, it was found that disabled workers actually typically received a higher return on their education than did nondisabled workers, *ceteris paribus*. The implication is that investment in disabled workers' education and training for high-paying jobs would go a long way to improving their compensation experience in the labor market and is consistent with the results found in Chapter 4. The analyses in Chapter 4 indicate that the distribution of disabled and nondisabled workers across occupations has actually become more dissimilar over time (with some recent improvements), with disabled individuals being significantly more concentrated in the lower-paying occupations. Workers with mental disorders are the most dissimilar in their distribution across occupations, compared with non-disabled workers.

The SSI and SSDI programs have a number of provisions that assist with training, rehabilitation, and educational attainment. The primary one is that benefit payments will continue while an individual is participating in a rehabilitation program, even if the recipient recovers from his or her disability. Recipients of SSI may also participate in what is called a PASS (Plan for Achieving Self-Support) program, under which a SSI recipient may put aside assets and money toward a plan that helps the recipient become self-sufficient, including rehabilitation or starting a business. These assets will be ignored in continuing determination of eligibility. In addition, the 1999 Ticket to Work legislation provides (as of December 2000) SSI and SSDI recipients with a "ticket" that can be used to obtain vocational rehabilitation, job or other support services from an employment network of the recipient's choice. This provision makes obtaining vocational rehabilitation more flexible, and thus more accessible.

In spite of such provisions, Chatterjee and Mitra (1998) indicate that less than 5 percent of federal spending for SSI and SSDI goes to training and rehabilitation. They suggest that this type of expenditure pattern on the disabled is the result of "a bias in disability programs in favor of short term equity considerations as opposed to the long run efficiency objectives" (p. 360). These authors also show that there is a positive link between enhancing a disabled person's human capital and his or her chances of participating in the labor market. The implication is that devoting more resources toward education and training would not only improve disabled workers' labor market experiences, but also help the bottom line of the SSI and SSDI programs by leading to more disabled people becoming self-sufficient.

In addition, the focus of SSI and SSDI on vocational rehabilitation may not direct resources where they will provide the greatest boost in compensation and occupational attainment outcomes for disabled workers. The growing earnings gap between those with and without college educations is well documented (for example, see Murphy, Juhn, and Pierce 1993). Training disabled workers for jobs requiring a college degree is an idea that has not received a great deal of attention. According to the results in Chapter 3, workers with musculoskeletal disorders appear to have suffered the most in terms of compensation. One reason for this may be that the cost of accommodating a worker's musculoskeletal disability in a blue-collar or physically-challenging position is likely much more expensive than if that worker became skilled in a less physically but more mentally demanding, and potentially higher-paying, job. Further evidence of the general lack of support for higher education is found in the income exclusion for earnings of disabled students. While attending school, students *only under the age of 22* are allowed to earn income that is excluded from calculating benefit eligibility and levels. This income exclusion could be extended to individuals over the age of 22 when they are working toward a terminal degree that would improve their occupational outcome.[6]

One area in which further general education for older SSI recipients is supported is in the development of a PASS; tuition, fees, books, and supplies for school are among those expenses that can be set aside as part of the SSI recipient's plan for self-support. While laudable, this provision is not likely to be very practical since it requires the SSI recipient, who is subject to strict earnings limitations, to set aside savings and assets that are likely difficult to acquire. An additional provision that allows the recipient to work (without penalty) while attending school may place attainment of higher education within the realm of financial possibility. The federal government does allow educational grants, fellowships, and scholarships used for tuition and fees to be excluded from earnings limitations. Portions of those sources used for room and board, however, are not currently excluded. A report by the Social Security Administration (2000) suggests that all portions of grants, scholarships, and fellowships be excluded from the earnings test.[7]

Given the importance of general education in improving the employment experience of disabled workers (as demonstrated in the analyses of this book), the federal government should explore the possibilities of providing more active support. One could also argue that if the basic goal is to improve the labor market experience of workers with disabilities, subsidized training and education should be made available to *all* disabled individuals, not only those affiliated with a government cash payment disability program. Improving the labor market experience of a single disabled worker could also provide externalities to the experience of other disabled workers. As employers and fellow workers become more comfortable working alongside the disabled and become more aware of such individuals' capabilities, even more doors would open to disabled workers who follow.

One policy change that seems to have had an unambiguous effect on the characteristics of jobs held by disabled workers is the extension of Medicaid and Medicare for SSI and SSDI recipients who have become ineligible for disability payments. Most part-time jobs do not offer health insurance, but many disabled workers may prefer part-time employment as a means of accommodation for their disability. Due to the extension of Medicaid and Medicare, disabled workers can now consider part-time employment without the risk of losing medical benefits. The results in Chapter 4 support this outcome; disabled workers are increasingly more likely to be employed part-time (versus full-time), but they are also increasingly more likely to be *voluntarily* (versus involuntarily) employed on a part-time basis. On the one hand, the extension of Medicaid and Medicare has opened up work opportunities that may improve a disabled worker's life. On the other hand, there is some evidence that part-time jobs are more likely to be marginal, temporary, unstable, and lower-paying (Blank 1990). The government might be able to provide assistance to (particularly, small) employers who want to explore flextime in order to accommodate workers' disabilities in occupations that may not be typical candidates for such scheduling, but that pay more and provide for advancement opportunities within the firm. One step that will likely contribute positively to this effort is the President's "New Freedom Initiative."[8] This concept calls for the fulfillment of the promise made by the government to people with disabilities through the passage of the ADA; it includes education, home ownership, access, and employment provisions. Expanding telecommuting opportunities is one example: "The Administration will provide Federal matching funds to states to guarantee low-interest loans for individuals with disabilities to purchase computers and other equipment necessary to telework from home. In addition, legislation will be proposed to make a company's contribution of computer and Internet access for home use by employees with disabilities a tax-free benefit."[9] Given the results in Chapter 4, that flexible work arrangements (i.e., part-time jobs) may be an important aspect of greater employment opportunities for people with disabilities, this proposal holds promise.

SCREENING AND MATCHING

The evidence of job separation and job search experiences of disabled workers presented in Chapter 5 is ambiguous. On the one hand, disabled workers search three weeks longer, on average, than similar nondisabled individuals before finding a job. On the other hand, job separations are less likely to be for involuntary reasons among disabled than among nondisabled workers, implying that disabled workers are not likely the "marginal" employees that some have speculated they are. While longer search spells are consistent with discriminatory hiring practices on the part of employers, the finding that most of the observed longer search spell is explained by individual characteristics suggests that endowments of disabled and nondisabled workers are being valued equally, but that employers go to greater lengths to discern the fit of a disabled worker's traits with a particular job. This care in hiring on the part of the employer would also lead to the lower probability that a separation is involuntary. In addition, the firm may have made some expenditures in accommodating the worker's disability and thus will be reluctant to lose that investment by laying off or firing the worker.

The lower probability that a separation is involuntary means that disabled workers experience a higher likelihood that a separation is voluntary. While this may be interpreted as disabled workers having a fair amount of mobility in the labor market, it may also mean that they have more difficulty than nondisabled individuals in finding a good job match. What is called for is a policy that assists employers in discerning the qualifications and fit of a disabled worker more quickly and that helps disabled workers in determining the appropriateness of a particular job. Measures for improving the efficacy and speed of job matches would include a clearing house at which employers could post job openings and workers could advertise skills (with appropriate accommodations); third-party certification of worker skills; and assistance with information (such as JAN) and with cost (such as tax credits) for accommodating a particular disability for the job to be filled.

The National Easter Seal Society provides many services that would facilitate matching of workers with employers. Skills evaluation and screening, employment skills training, and job placement services are among the programs offered through Easter Seals. JAN could also be expanded to provide job placement services, which it currently does not do.[10] The U.S. Office of Disability Employment Policy, however, has some initiatives that do assist in employment on a limited basis.[11] The Employer Assistance Referral Network (EARN) is designed to help employers in locating and recruiting qualified individuals with disabilities. The Workforce Recruitment Program is involved with securing summer employment and internships for students with disabilities, and Project EMPLOY is designed to expand and enhance job opportunities for people with cognitive disabilities by, primarily, providing funding to other organizations to provide employment services.

One thing that might be difficult for an employer to assess is the productivity of a disabled worker with accommodating equipment or services in place. If the government, or some private entity, could certify a particular skill (such as typing or editing) when a disabled individual has access to facilitating equipment, the employer would not be forced to bear the risk of hiring the worker and installing the necessary equipment without knowing what the outcome will be. There could be testing centers set up regionally, or mobile testing centers, that would contain the most common equipment needed for the worker to do the job in question.

THE ADA AND BEYOND

The labor market provisions of the ADA comprise a small part of the overall goals of the legislation. Furthermore, given the relatively low proportion of the disabled population that is actually in the labor force, and smaller yet that is employed, the potential impact of these provisions is not nearly as widespread as the effect of other elements of the legislation that cover aspects of a disabled person's life outside the labor market. As such, measuring the influence of the ADA on the overall quality of life of the disabled goes far beyond the potential impact on the labor market experience. Indeed, the key contributions of the ADA may be beyond quantification in economic terms; it is difficult to put a price on the dignity and respect that proponents might argue are among the most important dividends of the ADA.

Nevertheless, learning that the ADA did not result in dramatic, or even notable, improvement across multiple dimensions of the labor market experience of the disabled must be quite disappointing for the proponents of the legislation. In light of these findings, we are left with the question of why no such impact was forthcoming. One possible reason for legislation not having an effect on the intended beneficiaries is that there was nothing to improve: the disadvantaged are not really as disadvantaged as they might appear (because of factors the researcher may not be able to observe, for example). If this is the case, then the ADA is directed at a *nonexistent* target. A second possibility for finding no influence of the ADA on labor market outcomes among the disabled might be that the labor market provisions of the legislation are focused on the wrong things. Title I of the ADA is couched in terms of eliminating discriminatory behavior on the part of employers. It could be the case that discrimination is not the culprit determining inferior labor market outcomes for the disabled; in other words, the ADA is aiming at the *wrong* target. A third potential explanation for finding no impact is that the ADA is focused on the right target, but just *missed*. In other words, it may be the case that the legislation is ineffective, that employers are finding ways to get around the provisions and that workers are not able to exercise their rights under the law.

With the amount of evidence presented in this book, as well as that provided elsewhere, it is not likely that the ADA is aiming at a nonexistent target. One advantage of examining labor market outcomes from multiple dimensions, as was done here, is to be able to rule out numerous explanations for inferior labor market outcomes. The disabled clearly have further to go before enjoying labor market outcomes comparable to those experienced by the nondisabled. The possibility that the ADA has missed the target and that employers are able to somehow get around complying with the legislation is also not likely. The inability of employers to ignore the ADA is evidenced by the fact that disability claims made up 20 percent of all claims made to the EEOC during fiscal year 2001. This percentage was not too far behind the ratio of claims filed based on race (36 percent), sex (31 percent), and age (22 percent) during the same year and suggests that workers are aware of their rights and are holding employers accountable. The chance, then, that the ADA is aiming at the wrong target is still a possibility. While individual cases of discrimination (as evidenced by the number of EEOC claims) indicate that discrimination against disabled workers is likely occurring in the labor market, it still may not be the overwhelming determinant of inferior labor market outcomes. As suggested earlier in this chapter, other policies, such as promoting education and training, may go further toward improving labor market outcomes than a policy outlawing discrimination (which may only touch a small portion of the disabled).

Regardless of why the ADA does not seem to have affected the labor market experience of the disabled, this absence of impact begs the question of whether the ADA is necessary. Clearly, it is possible to argue the merits of the ADA on the ways in which it has likely improved the quality of life among the disabled beyond its labor market or quantifiable influence. However, even with regard to its labor market provisions, the ADA does serve as a statement of our social values, and it provides a legal mechanism with which to stem the activities of those who have not yet accepted those values. In addition, there is no question that it does serve to set the stage and to provide a labor market environment in which effective reforms, more narrowly focused on the needs of the disabled for improving outcomes, can be introduced.

Notes

1. See table of statistics titled, "Americans with Disabilities Act of 1990 (ADA) Charges FY1992–FY2001," found at <http://www.eeoc.gov/stats/ada-charges.html>.
2. See table of statistics titled, "Americans with Disabilities Act of 1900 (ADA) Charges FY1992–FY2001," found at <http://www.eeoc.gov/stats/ada-charges.html>.
3. Other possible explanations include the potential for the ADA to have a greater impact on overcoming negative social attitudes against people with mental disabilities (versus other types of disabilities) or improvements in medications occur-

ring during the same time period, which facilitated the labor market performance of people with mental disabilities.

4. More substantial architectural and transportation adaptation expenses can be deducted from tax liability by all businesses under IRS Code Section 190.

5. The web site for JAN is <http://www.jan.wvu.edu/>. Additional government resources for people with disabilities can be found at <http://www.disabilitydirect .gov>. The National Easter Seal Society (http://www.easter-seals.org/) also offers free information referral and suggestions for technological devices to help workers do their jobs.

6. This recommendation is also made by the Social Security Administration's March 2000 report to the Congress on income and resource exclusions. That report also recommends that the amount of earnings excluded be increased and then indexed to the CPI.

7. The report also suggests that grants, fellowships, and scholarships be excluded from resource limitations for nine months, based on the reality that many forms of financial aid are received at the beginning and paid out over the balance of the school year.

8. See the U.S. Health and Human Services Web site, "New Freedom Initiative: Fulfilling America's Promise to Americans with Disabilities," found at <http://www .hhs.gov/newfreedom/>.

9. See the U.S. Health and Human Services Web site, "New Freedom Initiative: Fulfilling America's Promise to Americans with Disabilities," found at <http://www .hhs.gov/newfreedom/>. Also see Chen (2001).

10. See note 5.

11. These job search and placement efforts (and others) can be located from the <http:// www.disabilitydirect.gov> Web site.

Appendix A

CPS Sample Construction

This appendix provides information regarding the use of the Current Population Survey data set for the analyses in this book. The lessons learned might be useful to others creating successive cross-sections across many years using the CPS. The notes and recommendations reflect the experience of the author only.

1. The complete set of outgoing rotation groups from the CPS was obtained from Unicon Research Corporation (http://www.unicon.com). The outgoing rotation group in the CPS consists of individuals in their 4th and 8th month of eight monthly interviews. A CPS respondent is interviewed for four consecutive months, not interviewed for four months, then interviewed again for four consecutive months. This source is highly recommended for not only outgoing rotation groups, but for all of the CPS data sets one might want. The data arrive on CDs with easy-to-use extraction software. The documentation is excellent; the coding across years is consistent; technical support is accessible and helpful; and the documentation also makes note of known data anomalies or errors. Unicon makes these data available for a fee.

2. The March supplemental files for each year were obtained from the Inter-University Consortium for Political and Social Research (ICPSR), <http://www.icpsr.umich.edu/>. We identified tremendous (un-correctable) problems with the 1994 March CPS obtained from ICPSR and ultimately obtained the data needed for 1994 from Unicon.

3. A variable of crucial importance to the analyses in this book is the indicator of disability status. That indicator is not available in the CPS public use file between 1981 and 1987; we contracted with the Census Bureau to extract the necessary variable and individual identifiers essential for matching with the rest of the CPS file for those years.

4. Creation of the CPS data sets for each year required matching individuals in each of the outgoing rotation groups from March, April, May, and June with the supplemental questionnaire in March. The match rate was approximately 90 percent for each month, except March, where the match rate, of course, was 100 percent.

5. The coding of the variable in the March supplement indicating whether an individual worked last year changed over the entire time period. Although this coding change is well documented, it could confound analyses if the difference is not noticed. Specifically, for 1981–1987, a "1" indicates that the

person did *not* work during the previous year, and, for 1988–1999, a "1" indicates that the person *did* work during the previous year.

6. Prior to 1994, the question of usual hours worked per week was asked of those who were earner eligible (outgoing rotation groups) and employed during the previous week. Starting in 1994, this variable was coded as zero for workers with variable hours, and the question regarding how many hours were worked at all jobs last week was changed to read, "Last week, how many hours did you actually work at your (main) job?" Unfortunately, the Census code book (which accompanies data from ICPSR) does not reflect the change in this question since 1994 (it still indicates that the question refers to hours worked at all jobs, when in fact, it now only reflects hours at the main job).

Appendix B

SIPP Sample Construction

In the terminology of the Survey of Income and Program Participation, a Panel refers to a group of interviewees and the year in which that group was first interviewed. A Wave refers to an interview within a Panel. Each Panel has anywhere from 3 (1989 Panel) to 12 (1996 Panel) interviews. Further details of the SIPP can be found on the Internet at <http://www.bls.census .gov/sipp/>. Core data from each Wave within a Panel used for sample construction were merged with the topical module for Wave 2 from the same Panel. Wave 2 topical modules were used for identification of a work disability for consistency over as many consecutive years as possible. When available, core data from Wave 2 in one Panel were combined with core data from Wave 5 in the previous Panel and with core data from Wave 8 in the Panel before that in order to construct a larger sample year. Table B.1 presents the layout of the SIPP sampling structure. The Waves merged across Panels (columns in Table B.1) are combined for illustration using a bold box outline. Since the goal was to create multiple cross sections comparable to the CPS, only Waves 2, 5, and 8 in each Panel were exploited.

Combining data across Panels was not possible for sample years 1986, 1989, 1990, 1995, 1996, and 1997 due to the lack of availability of overlapping Panels for which disability information is available. The labor market information, due to the rotation of sets of questions in the SIPP, corresponds to June of the year referenced. The exception to this pattern is the 1997 sample labor market information, which came from Wave 5 of the 1996 panel, which corresponds to August of 1997. Of course, these waves were merged with the disability topical module for that panel.

The disability check in the topical module was the variable used to designate a work-limiting disability. There are two checks in topical modules for the 1986–1993 Panels, but only one check in the 1996 Panel, resulting in the slightly smaller incidence of individuals with work-limiting disabilities in the 1996 and 1997 samples. The match rate across Waves within a Panel ranged from 81 to 89 percent success. Labor status refers to activity during the previous month (as opposed to the previous week, as in the CPS), since job information corresponds to activity over the month.

The primary usefulness of the SIPP derives from an ability to identify the *nature* of a disabled worker's disability. The categories identified are too numerous for all of them to be included in the analysis, so they are grouped into broad headings based on the classifications used by the Social Security Administration. Table B.2 shows how specific disabilities are classified.

Table B.1 SIPP Data Structure

		Panel										
Year	Month	1984	1985	1986	1987	1988	1989	1990	1991	1992	1993	1996
1983	Oct.	1										
1984	Feb.	2										
	June	3										
	Oct.	4										
1985	Feb.	5	1									
	June	6	2									
	Oct.	7	3									
1986	Feb.	8	4	1								
	June	9	5	**2**								
	Oct.		6	3								
1987	Feb.		7	4	1							
	June		8	**5**	**2**							
	Oct.			6	3							
1988	Feb.			7	4	1						
	June				**5**	**2**						
	Oct.				6	3						
1989	Feb.				7	4	1					
	June					**5**	2					
	Oct.					6	3					
1990	Feb.							1				
	June							**2**				
	Oct.							3				

<- 1986 sample
<- 1987 sample
<- 1988 sample
1989 sample ->
<- 1990 sample
<-Wave 2 (1989) top. mod. not avail.

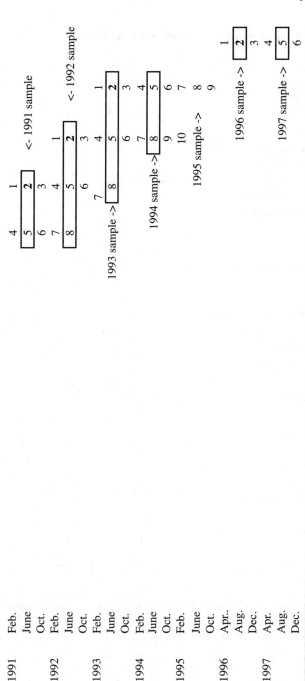

NOTE: Wave 2 topical module (number in bold) is where disability information is located. Waves bordered in bold are merged to create the sample year indicated. Each wave used for sample construction was merged with the Wave 2 topical module, then combined across panels as indicated. The 1996 panel continues for 12 waves through 1999, but only six were available at the time of analysis.

Table B.2 Classification of Disabilities in the SIPP Data Set

1. Musculoskeletal
Arthritis or rheumatism
Back or spine problems
Broken bone/fracture
Head or spinal cord injury
Hernia or spinal injury
Missing legs, feet, arms, hands, or fingers
Paralysis of any kind
Stiffness or deformity of the foot, leg, arm, or hand
Blindness or vision problems
Deafness or serious trouble hearing
Speech disorder

2. Internal systems
AIDS or AIDS-related condition
Cancer
Diabetes
Heart trouble, hardening of the arteries
High blood pressure
Kidney stones or chronic kidney trouble
Lung or respiratory problems
Stomach trouble
Thyroid trouble or goiter

3. Mental disorder
Alcohol or drug problem or disorder[a]
Learning disability
Mental or emotional problem or disorder
Mental retardation
Senility/dementia/Alzheimer's disease
Cerebral palsy
Epilepsy
Stroke
Tumor, cyst, or growth

4. Other

NOTE: Complete classification of disabilities by the Social Security Administration can be found at <http://www.ssa.gov/OP_Home/cfr20/404/404-ap09.htm>.
[a]Drug addiction is excluded from protection by the ADA.

Appendix C

Supplemental Tables

Table C.1 Trends in the Percentages of Total Sample and of Workers Indicating a Work-Limiting Disability, CPS Combined Outgoing Rotation Groups, 1981–2000

Year	% of sample	% of workers
1981	9.79	2.68
1982	10.19	2.69
1983	9.73	2.53
1984	10.20	2.74
1985	10.34	2.66
1986	9.89	2.68
1987	9.62	2.69
1988	9.15	2.63
1989	9.26	2.67
1990	9.34	2.74
1991	9.34	2.60
1992	9.44	2.70
1993	9.82	2.87
1994	10.95	2.68
1995	11.14	2.53
1996	10.88	2.73
1997	10.75	2.81
1998	10.05	2.51
1999	9.84	2.37
2000	9.99	2.70

Table C.2 Percentages of Disabled and Nondisabled Individuals Employed, CPS, 1981–2000

	Subsample employed (%)	
Year	Disabled	Nondisabled
1981	17.76	62.62
1982	17.27	61.39
1983	16.34	60.45
1984	17.21	62.93
1985	16.76	63.57
1986	17.70	63.79
1987	18.32	64.49
1988	19.11	63.98
1989	19.43	65.74
1990	19.35	65.98
1991	18.41	64.74
1992	18.88	64.39
1993	19.05	64.42
1994	16.50	66.16
1995	15.44	66.32
1996	16.41	66.71
1997	17.30	67.40
1998	17.09	67.88
1999	16.60	68.05
2000	17.15	68.70

Table C.3 Predicted Joint Probability of Labor Force Participation and Employment and Predicted Unconditional Employment Probability, by Disability Status, CPS, 1981–2000

	Average predicted probability			
	Nondisabled		Disabled	
	Being in the labor force and employed (1)	Employment (2)	Being in the labor force and employed (3)	Employment (4)
Year	Prob(LFP = 1, EMP = 1)	Prob(EMP = 1)	Prob(LFP = 1, EMP = 1)	Prob(EMP = 1)
1981	0.64271	0.84244	0.47840	0.79271
1982	0.62609	0.81519	0.47742	0.77384
1983	0.61727	0.79255	0.47474	0.76856
1984	0.64824	0.85387	0.50693	0.82802
1985	0.65675	0.85665	0.50837	0.82475
1986	0.66467	0.85364	0.51167	0.81465
1987	0.67498	0.86818	0.51993	0.83475
1988	0.68827	0.87833	0.53576	0.82908
1989	0.69070	0.88346	0.53884	0.85364
1990	0.69150	0.87427	0.52609	0.82427
1991	0.67530	0.84653	0.52123	0.81285
1992	0.67426	0.82397	0.51998	0.76743
1993	0.67738	0.83780	0.53733	0.80476
1994	0.68448	0.84973	0.49882	0.81405
1995	0.68820	0.87372	0.49520	0.83877
1996	0.69305	0.87742	0.50769	0.84971
1997	0.70309	0.87734	0.51408	0.84607
1998	0.71169	0.89380	0.51334	0.86027
1999	0.71529	0.89326	0.50755	0.83657
2000	0.72085	0.91141	0.52832	0.86493

NOTE: Estimates obtained from a bivariate probit model with selection. Regressors for both labor force and employment determination included the state unemployment rate; age; age squared; female, nonwhite, education, and regional dummies; and a disability dummy. The labor force participation equation also included nonlabor income, marital status, and a worked-last-year indicator. The employment equation included the number of weeks worked last year. The probabilities for each column are the average across the entire sample obtained by calculating the probability for each person (varying the disability dummy variable between 0 and 1), then averaging across the sample.

Table C.4 Relative Predicted Probabilities of Working in Each Firm Size, CPS 1987–1999

| Year | Ratio of predicted probabilities of a disabled worker relative to the predicted probability for a nondisabled coworker being employed by a firm by size | | |
	Small firm	Medium firm	Large firm
1987	1.1842	1.0756	0.9189
1988	1.1836	1.1063	0.9134
1989	1.1524	1.0403	0.9409
1990	1.1372	1.0174	0.9507
1991	1.1682	0.9417	0.9493
1992	1.2127	0.8759	0.9501
1993	1.0873	1.0410	0.9512
1994	1.0567	0.9999	0.9787
1995	1.1772	0.9384	0.9399
1996	1.1811	0.8598	0.9575
1997	1.1341	0.9900	0.9511
1998	1.0110	0.9319	1.0106
1999	1.0963	0.9840	0.9675
Change over time period	−0.0879	−0.0917	0.0487

NOTE: Small firms have fewer than 25 employees; medium firms have 25–99 employees; and large firms have 100 or more employees. Regressors (in addition to a disability dummy variable) in the multinomial logit regression included age; age squared; and regional, education, female, nonwhite, and central city dummy variables.

Table C.5 Observed and Selectivity-Corrected Wage Differentials, CPS, 1981–2000

Year	Observed wage differential[a]	Wage differential corrected for selectivity into the labor market[b]	Endowment effect[c]	Coefficient effect[d]	Selection effect[e]
1981	0.1587	0.1315	0.0386	0.0929	0.0272
1982	0.1294	0.1318	0.0307	0.1011	−0.0024
1983	0.1717	0.1991	0.0056	0.1935	−0.0275
1984	0.1885	0.1902	0.0312	0.1590	−0.0017
1985	0.1706	0.2037	0.0476	0.1561	−0.0332
1986	0.1948	0.2144	0.0634	0.1510	−0.0197
1987	0.2008	0.2342	0.0591	0.1751	−0.0334
1988	0.2089	0.1954	0.0436	0.1518	0.0135
1989	0.2512	0.2009	0.0766	0.1243	0.0503
1990	0.2469	0.2605	0.0807	0.1798	−0.0136
1991	0.2649	0.2494	0.0769	0.1725	0.0154
1992	0.2644	0.2901	0.0890	0.2011	−0.0258
1993	0.2723	0.3114	0.0852	0.2262	−0.0391
1994	0.2733	0.3337	0.0911	0.2427	−0.0605
1995	0.2400	0.2768	0.0792	0.1976	−0.0368
1996	0.2638	0.2642	0.0929	0.1713	−0.0004
1997	0.2117	0.2090	0.0791	0.1299	0.0027
1998	0.2843	0.2776	0.0884	0.1892	0.0066
1999	0.2941	0.3028	0.0881	0.2147	−0.0087
2000	0.2809	0.2566	0.0674	0.1892	0.0243

NOTE: The first-stage probit estimation included the following regressors: age; age squared; nonwhite, female, disabled, single household, education, and worked-last-year dummy variables; and nonlabor income. Regressions for 1981 and 1982 do not include a union dummy. Second-stage wage estimations included the following regressors: hour of work; age; age squared; and union, female, single household, nonwhite, education, region, industry, occupation, and government dummy variables. Regressions for 1983 do not include dummies for the service; farming, fishing, and forestry; or the craft occupations due to the absence of representation of disabled workers in these occupations in the sample. $\hat{\beta}_{nd}$ (coefficients from the nondisabled estimation) was used to represent the "nondiscriminatory" world since the disabled make up such a small proportion of the whole.

[a] $\overline{\ln W_{nd}} - \overline{\ln W_d}$

[b] $\overline{\ln W_{nd}} - \overline{\ln W_d} - [(\hat{c}_{nd}\overline{\lambda}_{nd}) - (\hat{c}_d\overline{\lambda}_d)]$

[c] $\hat{\beta}_{nd}(\overline{X}_{nd} - \overline{X}_d)$

[d] $\overline{X}_d(\beta_{nd} - \beta_d)$

[e] $[(\hat{c}_{nd}\overline{\lambda}_{nd}) - (\hat{c}_d\overline{\lambda}_d)]$.

Table C.6 Marginal Effect of Being Disabled on the Probability of Employer-Provided Health Insurance and of Being Included in the Employer's Pension Plan, CPS

Year	Measure of earnings not included in probit estimation		Measure of earnings included in probit estimation	
	$\dfrac{\partial\Phi(\text{HealthIns})}{\partial\text{Disabled}}$	$\dfrac{\partial\Phi(\text{Pension})}{\partial\text{Disabled}}$	$\dfrac{\partial\Phi(\text{HealthIns})}{\partial\text{Disabled}}$	$\dfrac{\partial\Phi(\text{Pension})}{\partial\text{Disabled}}$
1980	−0.0848	−0.0890	—	—
	(0.0094)	(0.0098)		
1981	−0.0859	−0.0924	—	—
	(0.0096)	(0.0100)		
1982	−0.0888	−0.0751	—	—
	(0.0101)	(0.0104)		
1983	−0.0822	−0.0835	—	—
	(0.0099)	(0.0102)		
1984	−0.0740	−0.0677	—	—
	(0.0098)	(0.0100)		
1985	−0.0861	−0.0849	—	—
	(0.0098)	(0.0102)		
1986	−0.0956	−0.0824	—	—
	(0.0099)	(0.0103)		
1987	−0.0850	−0.0901	−0.0243	−0.0356
	(0.0100)	(0.0105)	(0.0096)	(0.0101)
1988	−0.0990	−0.0911	−0.0428	−0.0402
	(0.0099)	(0.0104)	(0.0095)	(0.0100)
1989	−0.0891	−0.0820	−0.0315	−0.0285
	(0.0095)	(0.0097)	(0.0091)	(0.0093)
1990	−0.1050	−0.0900	−0.0415	−0.0347
	(0.0099)	(0.0101)	(0.0095)	(0.0097)
1991	−0.1150	−0.1059	−0.0626	−0.0595
	(0.0099)	(0.0101)	(0.0095)	(0.0097)
1992	−0.1188	−0.0967	−0.0638	−0.0462
	(0.0101)	(0.0101)	(0.0098)	(0.0097)
1993	−0.0741	−0.0856	−0.0329	−0.0424
	(0.0100)	(0.0102)	(0.0097)	(0.0098)
1994	−0.0831	−0.0872	−0.0380	−0.0450
	(0.0107)	(0.0108)	(0.0104)	(0.0105)
1995	−0.1070	−0.1210	−0.0869	−0.1045
	(0.0105)	(0.0108)	(0.0105)	(0.0108)
1996	−0.1159	−0.1281	−0.0970	−0.1094
	(0.0104)	(0.0108)	(0.0104)	(0.0107)

Table C.6 (continued)

Year	Measure of earnings not included in probit estimation		Measure of earnings included in probit estimation	
	$\dfrac{\partial\Phi(\text{HealthIns})}{\partial\text{Disabled}}$	$\dfrac{\partial\Phi(\text{Pension})}{\partial\text{Disabled}}$	$\dfrac{\partial\Phi(\text{HealthIns})}{\partial\text{Disabled}}$	$\dfrac{\partial\Phi(\text{Pension})}{\partial\text{Disabled}}$
1997	−0.1101	−0.1110	−0.0913	−0.0944
	(0.0109)	(0.0113)	(0.0109)	(0.0112)
1998	−0.1018	−0.1022	−0.0822	−0.0828
	(0.0111)	(0.0115)	(0.0111)	(0.0114)
1999	−0.0728	−0.1036	−0.0526	−0.0832
	(0.0108)	(0.0111)	(0.0107)	(0.0110)

NOTE: A reliable earnings variable was not available in the years 1981–1987. Regressors in the probit estimation included nonwhite, female, education, single household, government, industry, occupation, and disabled dummy variables; age; age squared; earnings from the job; and usual hours worked. Standard errors for the partial derivatives are in parentheses.
Φ is the standard normal cumulative distribution function.

Table C.7 Impact of Being Disabled on the Probability of Part-Time and Voluntary Part-Time Employment, CPS, 1981–2000

	Predicted marginal effect of a disability on probability	
Year	Being employed part-time[a] (1)	Being voluntarily employed part-time[b] (2)
1981	0.0557	−0.0030
1982	0.0581	−0.0010
1983	0.0836	−0.0643
1984	0.0665	−0.0098
1985	0.0664	−0.0744
1986	0.0850	−0.0145
1987	0.0594	−0.0085
1988	0.0820	−0.0399
1989	0.0924	0.0067
1990	0.0824	−0.0214
1991	0.0844	−0.0367
1992	0.0886	0.0053
1993	0.1134	0.0173
1994	0.1425	0.0365
1995	0.1227	0.0187
1996	0.1380	0.0266
1997	0.1492	0.0676
1998	0.1407	0.0385
1999	0.1569	0.0594
2000	0.1250	0.0182

NOTE: The marginal effects are calculated at the sample means, except disability status, which is varied between 0 and 1 to generate the marginal effect. See Long (1997).

[a] Predicted marginal effects in column 1 result from estimation of a bivariate model of employment and part-time employment, accounting for selection at the employment stage. Regressors in both the employment and part-time employment equations included age, education, region, race, gender, marital status, and a central city residence indicator. Regressors unique to the employment equation included the state unemployment rate and the number of weeks worked last year. Regressors unique to the part-time employment equation included occupation and industry dummies, nonlabor income, and a government employer indicator.

[b] Predicted marginal effects in column 2 result from estimation of a univariate probit model of the probability of being voluntarily employed part-time. The sample is restricted to all part-time workers, so results are not generalizable beyond this sample. Voluntary part-time is defined as did not want to work full time (1994–1999), and the reason for working under 35 hours per week (1981–1993) was coded as 07–15 (see Chapter 4, Note 8, and Stratton 1994). Regressors included age, education, region, race, gender, marital status, nonlabor income, and occupation dummies, industry dummies, a government employer dummy, and an indicator of whether the person worked last year or not.

Table C.8 The Duncan Index as a Measure of Dissimilarity in Distribution of Workers across Occupations and Industries, CPS, 1981–2000

Year	Disabled vs. nondisabled		Nonwhite vs. white	
	Occupation	Industry	Occupation	Industry
1981	0.1251	0.0443	0.1514	0.1063
1982	0.1065	0.0438	0.1648	0.1081
1983	**0.1077**	0.0602	**0.1588**	0.0923
1984	0.1089	0.0514	0.1528	0.1029
1985	0.1141	0.0394	0.1590	0.1018
1986	0.1455	0.0630	0.1570	0.0915
1987	0.1340	0.0602	0.1430	0.0770
1988	0.1188	0.0670	0.1492	0.0902
1989	0.1431	0.0472	0.1375	0.0885
1990	0.1351	0.0518	0.1357	0.0871
1991	0.1447	0.0878	0.1323	0.0822
1992	0.1506	0.0475	0.1407	0.0711
1993	0.1442	0.0425	0.1247	0.0838
1994	0.1474	0.0684	0.1173	0.0745
1995	0.1336	0.0425	0.1239	0.0754
1996	0.1340	0.0854	0.1264	0.0724
1997	0.1273	0.0682	0.1210	0.0726
1998	0.1316	0.0782	0.1055	0.0693
1999	0.1467	0.0562	0.1107	0.0805
2000	0.1236	0.0771	0.1082	0.0851

NOTE: The Duncan Index reflects the % of workers in the labor market that would have to switch occupation or industry in order to equalize the distribution of workers in both groups across occupations or industries. The index is calculated as

$$D = \frac{1}{2} \sum_{j=1}^{K} |a_j - b_j|,$$ where K is the number of occupations (industries), and a and b refer to the proportion of the two different groups of interest in occupation/industry j (e.g., a is the proportion of nondisabled workers in occupation/industry j, and b is the proportion of disabled workers in occupation/industry j). The numbers in bold represent projections replacing the actual calculated index for that year, which was clearly an outlier.

Table C.9 Disabled and Nondisabled Job Separators by Reason for Job Separation (%), CPS, 1981–2000

Year	Nondisabled			Disabled		
	Voluntary (%)	Involuntary (%)	Other (%)	Voluntary (%)	Involuntary (%)	Other (%)
1981	66.42	19.09	14.50	82.30	8.35	9.36
1982	66.39	19.50	14.11	81.13	11.21	7.66
1983	66.21	20.11	13.68	81.04	10.07	8.89
1984	66.05	19.92	14.03	80.42	10.49	9.09
1985	66.28	18.55	15.16	78.13	11.44	10.43
1986	67.32	18.68	13.99	80.58	9.68	9.74
1987	68.57	17.71	13.72	80.49	10.21	9.30
1988	68.96	17.43	13.61	80.99	9.87	9.14
1989	69.89	24.44	5.67	82.01	12.90	5.09
1990	69.83	24.11	6.06	80.68	14.02	5.30
1991	63.05	30.65	6.30	79.37	14.49	6.14
1992	61.55	32.75	5.70	76.46	18.29	5.25
1993	62.09	31.62	6.30	78.31	16.98	4.71
1994	56.54	36.97	6.49	60.98	33.07	5.94
1995	56.20	36.46	7.34	57.99	31.07	10.95
1996	56.36	35.96	7.68	52.92	36.77	10.31
1997	58.55	33.13	8.32	57.19	33.09	9.71
1998	58.89	33.36	7.75	58.27	29.92	11.81
1999	58.73	32.64	8.63	68.72	26.43	4.85
2000	60.95	30.81	8.24	63.64	27.27	9.09

NOTE: Voluntary separations included the following reasons: personal, family, school; personal/family (includes pregnancy); return to school; health; retirement/old age; and unsatisfactory work arrangements (hours/pay/etc.). Involuntary separations included the following reasons: seasonal job completed, temporary seasonal or intermittent job completed, slack work/business, and temporary nonseasonal job completed. Sample sizes for the years 1994–1998 were considerably smaller than in earlier years due to a change in respondents for job separation questions. Prior to 1994, questions were asked of those who worked in the past five years; after 1994, only those who worked in the past 12 months were asked job separation questions.

Table C.10 Probability of an Employment Separation Being Voluntary and Involuntary by Disability Status, CPS, 1981–2000

	Probability			
	Voluntary separation		Involuntary separation	
Year	Disabled	Nondisabled	Disabled	Nondisabled
1981	0.8153	0.6767	0.0786	0.1868
1982	0.7989	0.6816	0.1113	0.1879
1983	0.8052	0.6794	0.0950	0.1921
1984	0.8032	0.6803	0.0952	0.1887
1985	0.7751	0.6854	0.1111	0.1740
1986	0.8056	0.6960	0.0903	0.1727
1987	0.8060	0.7067	0.0903	0.1646
1988	0.8089	0.7073	0.0901	0.1648
1989	0.8496	0.7216	0.1011	0.2219
1990	0.8479	0.7271	0.1067	0.2135
1991	0.8144	0.6655	0.1240	0.2708
1992	0.8067	0.6382	0.1395	0.3057
1993	0.8090	0.6456	0.1428	0.2911
1994	0.7115	0.5848	0.2287	0.3514
1995	0.6811	0.5768	0.2134	0.3498
1996	0.6506	0.5843	0.2532	0.3373
1997	0.7068	0.6145	0.2019	0.2997
1998	0.6533	0.6091	0.2238	0.3133
1999	0.7940	0.6121	0.1621	0.2990
2000	0.7346	0.6338	0.1748	0.2794

NOTE: See notes to table C.9 for definitions of voluntary and involuntary. The characteristics (other than disability) for which the probabilities were calculated were the means corresponding to the entire sample. See Long (1997). Regressions for 1981, 1982, and 1983 contain more limited industry and occupation classifications. Regressors included in the multinomial logit analysis included age; age squared; number of weeks worked last year; and industry, occupation, education, female, nonwhite, single, central city, region, and disability dummy variables.

Table C.11 Probability of an Unemployment Spell Being the Result of Losing a Job, Leaving a Job, Reentering the Labor Force, or Newly Entering the Labor Force, by Disability Status, CPS, 1989–2000

	Probability							
	Job loser		Job leaver		Reentrant		New entrant	
Year	Disabled	Non-disabled	Disabled	Non-disabled	Disabled	Non-disabled	Disabled	Non-disabled
1989	0.4346	0.4890	0.1459	0.1601	0.3974	0.3315	0.0221	0.0194
1990	0.3980	0.5174	0.1753	0.1536	0.4085	0.3081	0.0182	0.0208
1991	0.5041	0.6294	0.1873	0.1283	0.2988	0.2297	0.0099	0.0126
1992	0.5121	0.6721	0.1299	0.1032	0.3474	0.2150	0.0106	0.0096
1993	0.4925	0.6120	0.1671	0.1235	0.3280	0.2535	0.0123	0.0110
1994	0.3996	0.5155	0.1425	0.0975	0.4546	0.3849	0.0033	0.0020
1995	0.4094	0.5358	0.0994	0.1080	0.4780	0.3497	0.0132	0.0065
1996	0.4947	0.5246	0.0681	0.1082	0.4342	0.3647	0.0029	0.0025
1997	0.3269	0.4712	0.0625	0.1180	0.5826	0.4017	0.0280	0.0091
1998	0.4399	0.5030	0.1380	0.1165	0.4192	0.3773	0.0029	0.0032
1999	0.2005	0.4736	0.1852	0.1410	0.6127	0.3844	0.0015	0.0010
2000	0.3662	0.4757	0.1587	0.1393	0.4695	0.3811	0.0055	0.0039

NOTE: The characteristics (other than disability) for which the probabilities were calculated are the means corresponding to the entire sample. See Long (1997). Regressors in the multinomial logit analysis included age; age squared; number of weeks worked last year; number of weeks looking last year; and female, single, nonwhite, education, central city, region, and disability dummy variables.

Table C.12 Mean Difference in Expected Duration and Predicted Expected Duration across Disability Status, CPS, 1981–2000

Year	Mean difference in expected duration across disability status (weeks) (1)	Predicted expected duration (weeks)	
		Disabled (2)	Nondisabled (3)
1981	8.72	24.18	24.20
1982	11.84	27.92	26.79
1983	12.96	37.14	34.43
1984	12.40	31.44	30.52
1985	16.74	33.40	25.55
1986	20.12	26.20	24.57
1987	23.54	32.75	24.81
1988	19.10	25.88	22.07
1989	13.04	26.69	20.81
1990	12.94	22.37	20.56
1991	16.82	27.60	23.82
1992	5.42	32.17	30.84
1993	15.62	36.46	30.25
1994	11.24	37.68	39.56
1995	18.70	41.87	34.27
1996	17.74	47.71	34.19
1997	14.24	32.44	31.81
1998	0.66	22.39	30.03
1999	19.68	32.39	27.90
2000	3.78	30.60	27.64

NOTE: Mean expected duration (used to calculate the difference shown in column 1) is calculated as two times the observed censored search duration at a given point in time, as advocated by Akerlof and Main (1981); this results in a valid representation of completed search spells under the assumption of a steady state. Predicted expected duration (columns 2 and 3) was calculated using coefficient estimates resulting from the estimation of an accelerated failure time model where search duration is assumed to be distributed as a Weibull: $E[t_i | t_i > 0; X_i, \beta, \sigma] = \exp(X_i\beta)\Gamma(1+\sigma)$. See the text to Chapter 5 for definition of terms. The characteristics (other than disability) for which the predicted expected durations were calculated (X) are the means corresponding to the entire sample. See Long (1997). Regressors for the duration analysis included age; age squared; non-labor income; female, single, nonwhite, education, and regional dummies; dummy variables for availability to work, whether searcher wanted a full-time job, and whether searcher worked last year; and dummy variables for search methods (private agency, public agency, checked with friends, checked with employer, and checked ads), disability status, and search methods interacted with disability status.

Appendix D

State Disability Legislation

Table D.1 State Disability Legislation

State	Legislation	Current covered employer, definitions of disability, and exceptions
Alabama	Title 21 Handicapped Persons, Acts 1975, Chapter 7 Rights of Blind and Otherwise Physically Disabled Persons Source: Michie's Alabama Code 1975, Volume 14A, 1997 Replacement Volume.	No definitions available
Alaska	Title 18 Health, Safety, and Housing, Chapter 80 State Commission for Human Rights, Article 4 Discriminatory Practices Prohibited Language referring to disability added in 1987 Source: Alaska Statutes 1962, Volume 5 (1998).	Employer: person including state, political subdivision of state, one or more employees Disability: physical or mental impairment that substantially limits one or more major life activities; a history of, or a misclassification as having such; an impairment treated as a limitation, regarded by others as such; condition requiring use of prosthesis, special equipment or service animal Exclusions: fraternity, charitable, educational, or religious associations or corporations, if not organized for private profit, domestic employment

Table D.1 (continued)

State	Legislation	Current covered employer, definitions of disability, and exceptions
Arizona	Title 41 State Government, Chapter 9 Civil Rights, Article 4 Discrimination in Employment Language referring to disability added in 1985 Source: Arizona Revised Statutes Annotated, Volume 12B (1999).	Employer: has 15 or more employees, working for 20 or more calendar weeks Disability: a physical impairment, a record of physical impairment, being regarded as having a physical impairment Exclusions: U.S. government, departments, agencies; corporations, Indian tribes; private associations; employers of aliens; religious entities
Arkansas	Title 16 Practice, Procedure, and Courts, Subtitle 7 Particular Proceedings and Remedies, Chapter 123 Civil Rights, Subchapter 1 The Arkansas Civil Rights Act of 1993 Source: Arkansas Code of 1987 Annotated, 1999 Supplement Volume 16. Title 20 Public Health and Welfare, Chapter 14 Disabled People, Subchapter 3 Rights General, Section 301 Policy (public employers only) Source: Arkansas Code of 1987 Annotated, 2000 Replacement Volume 20 A.	Employer: employs nine or more employees, 20 or more calendar weeks Disability: a physical or mental impairment that substantially limits a major life function Exclusions: employment by a religious corporation, association, society, or other religious entity, family employment

Table D.1 (continued)

State	Legislation	Current covered employer, definitions of disability, and exceptions
California	Title 2 Government of the State of California, Division 3 Part 2.8 Department of Fair Employment and Housing Article added in 1980 Source: West's Annotated California Codes—Government Code, Sections 12300–14599 (1992).	Employer: regularly employs five or more persons or representative agents, the state, political or civil subdivision thereof, and cities; for purposes of mental disability, employs 15 or more persons Disability: includes mental and psychological disorder; health impairment affecting the body systems, or limits an individual's ability to participate in major life activities; other health impairment requiring special education or related services; being regarded as having or having had such health impairment; being regarded as having or having had such health impairment that may become a disability Exclusions: religious organizations and not-for-profit private corporations, family employment

Table D.1 (continued)

State	Legislation	Current covered employer, definitions of disability, and exceptions
Colorado	Administrative and Organization Act of 1968 Title 24 Government—State, Article 34 Department of Regulatory Services, Part 3 Colorado Civil Rights Division—Commission—Procedures and Part 4 Employment Practices Physical impairment provision was in place in 1979; amended after July 1, 1992, to include mental impairment for different articles Source: Colorado Revised Statutes 1997, Volume 7.	Employer: state of Colorado and any political subdivision, commission, institution, or school district thereof, every other person employing persons within the state Disability: physical impairment which substantially limits one or more of a person's major life activities, includes record of and being regarded as having such an impairment; mental impairment means mental or psychological disorder Exclusions: religious organizations except those supported by public funds, domestic employment
Connecticut	Title 46a Human Rights, Chapter 814c Human Rights and Opportunities In 1973 discrimination based on physical disability including blindness was made unfair employment practice Source: Connecticut General Statutes Annotated, Volume 21B (1995).	Employer: includes state and political divisions and any person/employer with three or more persons in employ Disability: any individual who has any chronic physical handicap, infirmity, or impairment Exclusions: family employment, domestic service

Table D.1 (continued)

State	Legislation	Current covered employer, definitions of disability, and exceptions
Delaware	Title 19 Labor, Chapter 7 Employment Practices, Subchapter 3 Handicapped Persons Employment Protections Handicapped section added on July 11, 1988 Source: Delaware Code Annotated, Revised 1974, Volume 11, 1995 Replacement Volume. Title 16 Health and Safety, Chapter 95, Delaware White Cane Law, Section 9501 Public Safety; White Cane Day (public employers only) Source: Delaware Code Annotated, Revised 1974, Volume 9, 1995, Replacement Volume.	Employer: state or any political subdivision, or board, department, commission or school district thereof, and any person employing 20 or more persons, 20 or more calendar weeks Disability: having physical or mental impairment which substantially limits one or more major life activities, has a record of such or is regarded as having such an impairment Exclusions: agriculture, domestic employment, family employment
Florida	Title XLIV Civil Rights, Chapter 760 Discrimination in the Treatment of Persons; Minority Representation, Part 1 Florida Civil Rights Act Provided for discrimination based on handicap in 1977 Source: West's Florida Statutes Annotated, Volume 21A (1997).	Employer: person employing 15 or more employees, 20 or more calendar weeks, any agent for such a person No other definitions available

Table D.1 (continued)

State	Legislation	Current covered employer, definitions of disability, and exceptions
Georgia	Title 34, Chapter 6A Equal Employment for Persons with Disabilities Act passed in 1981 Source: Official Code of Georgia Annotated, Volume 21, 1998 Edition. Title 45, Chapter 19 Labor Practices, Article 2 Fair Employment Practices Act passed in 1978 (public employers only) Source: Official Code of Georgia Annotated, Volume 33, 1990 Edition.	Employer: person or governmental unit or officer, or agent of an employer, having 15 or more individuals employed, 20 or more calendar weeks Disability: any condition or characteristic that renders a person an individual with disabilities Exclusions: no exclusions available
Hawaii	Title 21 Labor and Industrial Relations, Chapter 378 Employment Practices, Part 1 Discriminatory Practices Initially passed in 1981 with reference to physical handicap Source: Hawaii Revised Statutes, Volume 7, 1993 Replacement.	Employer: any person, including state or political subdivisions, any agent of such a person, having one or more employees Disability: the state of having a physical or mental impairment which substantially limits one or more major life activities, having a record of such an impairment, or being regarded as having such an impairment Exclusions: U.S. government, religious organizations

Table D.1 (continued)

State	Legislation	Current covered employer, definitions of disability, and exceptions
Idaho	Title 67 State Government and State Affairs, Chapter 59, Commission on Human Rights Language added in 1988 referring to handicap Source: Idaho Code, Volume 11 (1995). Title 56 Public Assistance and Welfare, Chapter 7 Rights of Blind and Physically Handicapped Persons, Section 56–707 Initially passed in 1969 (public employers only) Source: Idaho Code, Volume 10 (1999).	Employer: person who hires 5 or more employees, 20 or more calendar weeks Disability: physical or mental condition which constitutes a substantial limitation to that person, person with disability is one with such a disability, has record of such, or is regarded as having such a disability Exclusions: domestic employment, religious organizations
Illinois	Chapter 775 Human Rights, Act 5 Illinois Human Rights Act Effective July 1, 1980, with handicapped provisions in place Source: West's Illinois Smith and Hurd Illinois Compiled Statutes Annotated, Chapter 765 to 799(1993).	Employer: employs 15 or more employees, 20 or more calendar weeks, employing one or more employees when a handicap discriminatory complaint is made, without regard to number of employees for governmental unit or agency, or any party to a public contract Disability: determinable physical or mental characteristic of a person which is unrelated to a person's ability to perform a particular job or position Exclusions: religious entities, domestic servants, elected public officials (as employers)

Table D.1 (continued)

State	Legislation	Current covered employer, definitions of disability, and exceptions
Indiana	Title 22 Labor and Industrial Safety, Article 9 Civil Rights, Chapter 5 Employment Discrimination against Disabled Persons Handicap language added in 1975 Source: Burns Indiana Statutes Annotated, Title 22, Articles 4–15, 1997 Replacement Volume.	Employer: state or any political or civil subdivision thereof and any person engaged in industry affecting commerce having 15 or more employees, 20 calendar weeks Disability: physical or mental impairment that substantially limits at least one of the major life activities, a record of an impairment or being regarded as having an impairment Exclusions: U.S. government or corporation owned by the government of the U.S.A. or an Indian tribe, and a private membership club other than labor organization, religious corporation

Table D.1 (continued)

State	Legislation	Current covered employer, definitions of disability, and exceptions
Iowa	Title VI Human Services, Subtitle 1 Social Justice and Human Rights, Chapter 216 Civil Rights Commission, Section 216.6 Unfair Employment Practices Iowans with Disabilities Act 1995	Employer: state, political subdivision board, commission, department, institution, or school district thereof, and every other person employing employees within the state
	Ch. 216 was transferred from Ch. 601A, Civil Rights Commission, Code 1991	Disability: physical or mental condition of a person which constitutes a substantial handicap; extends definition of disabled to include HIV / AIDS person
	Legislation initially passed in 1972	
	Source: Iowa Code Annotated, Volume 10A, 1999 Cumulative Annual Pocket Part.	Exclusions: employers with fewer than 4 employees, family employment, personal service to person of the employer and religious entities
	Title VI Human Services, Subtitle 1 Social Justice and Human Rights, Chapter 216 C Rights of Blind, Partially Blind and Physically Disabled Persons, Section 216C.1, 216C.2	
	Transferred from Ch. 601D Rights of Blind and Physically Disabled, Code of 1991	
	In place by 1971 (public employers only)	
	Source: Iowa Code Annotated, Volume 10A, 1994.	

Table D.1 (continued)

State	Legislation	Current covered employer, definitions of disability, and exceptions
Kansas	Chapter 44 Labor and Industries, Article 10 Kansas Acts against Discrimination Included physical handicap in 1974 Source: Kansas Statutes Annotated, Volume 3A (1993).	Employer: any person in the state employing four or more persons, includes any person acting directly or indirectly for an employer, labor organizations, nonsectarian corporations, organizations engaged in social work and the state and political and municipal subdivisions; excludes nonprofit fraternal or social associations or corporations Disability: a physical or mental impairment that substantially limits one or more of the major life activities of an individual, a record of such or being regarded as having such an impairment Exclusions: family employment and domestic service

Table D.1 (continued)

State	Legislation	Current covered employer, definitions of disability, and exceptions
Kentucky	Title 27 Labor and Human Rights, Chapter 344 Civil Rights Disability provision effective in 1992 Source: Michie's Kentucky Revised Statutes, Volume 12A, 1997 Replacement. Title 17 Economic Security and Public Welfare, Chapter 207 Aid to the Needy Blind—Equal Opportunities, Section150 Prohibited Employment Practices—Exceptions Disability section added in 1976 (public employers only) Source: Michie's Kentucky Revised Statutes, Volume 8B, 1998 Replacement.	Employer: person engaged in an industry affecting commerce who has 15 or more employees, at least 20 weeks per year for purposes of disability discrimination and any agent of that person; otherwise 8 weeks Disability: physical or mental impairment that substantially limits one or more of the major life activities of an individual, a record of such or being regarded as having such an impairment Exclusions: U.S. government, U.S. government corporation, Indian tribe, bona fide private membership club
Louisiana	Title 23 Labor and Workers' Compensation, Chapter 3-A Prohibited Discrimination in Employment, Part III Disability Legislation initially passed in 1980 Source: West's Louisiana Statutes Revised Annotated, Volume 15D (1998).	Employer: employs 15 or more employees, 20 or more calendar weeks; refers to person, association, legal or commercial entity, state and its agencies receiving services from an employee and giving compensation in return Disability: any person with physical or mental impairment limiting one or more of the major life activities, or has record of such, or is regarded as having such an impairment Exclusions: family or domestic employment

Table D.1 (continued)

State	Legislation	Current covered employer, definitions of disability, and exceptions
Maine	Title 5, Administrative Procedures and Services, Part 12 Human Rights, Chapter 337 Human Rights Act, Subchapter 3, Fair Employment Physical handicap language in place in 1973 Source: Maine Revised Statutes Annotated, Volume 2A, Title 5, 1998 Supplementary Pamphlet.	Employer: includes any person in the state employing any number of employees, whatever the place of employment, and any person outside this state whose employees' place of employment is within the state; labor organization Disability: has physical or mental disability, has a record of or is regarded as having a physical or mental disability Exclusions: none for purposes of disability
Maryland	Article 49B Human Relations Commission, Discrimination in Employment Disability language added in 1974 Source: Michie's Annotated Code of Maryland 1957, Volume 4, 1999 Supplement.	Employer: a person engaged in an industry or business with 15 or more employees, 20 or more calendar weeks, includes state Disability: any physical disability, infirmity, malformation or disfigurement, and any mental impairment or deficiency Exclusions: bona fide private membership club; elected public officials, their chosen personnel staff, appointee, or immediate advisor (as employees)

Table D.1 (continued)

State	Legislation	Current covered employer, definitions of disability, and exceptions
Massachusetts	Chapter 151B Unlawful Discrimination because of race, color, religious creed, national origin, ancestry or sex In 1983 added language and section to include discrimination against handicapped Source: Massachusetts General Laws Annotated, Volume 22A Chapter 151–151E (1996).	Employer: employs six or more persons, the commonwealth and all political subdivisions, boards, departments and commissions thereof Disability: physical or mental impairment which substantially limits one or more major life activities of a person, a record of such or being regarded as having such impairment Exclusions: social clubs, private nonprofit organizations, religious organizations, family and domestic employment
Michigan	Chapter 37 Civil Rights, Persons with Disabilities Civil Rights Act, Article 2 Employment Act passed in 1976 Source: Michigan Compiled Laws, 1999 Cumulative Annual Pocket Part.	Employer: any person who has one or more employees, includes contractor/ subcontractor to state/ government entity Disability: a determinable physical or mental characteristic of an individual substantially limiting one or more of the major life activities of that individual and is unrelated to the individual's abilities to perform the duties of a particular job or position, qualifications for employment or promotion; a history of such or being regarded as having a determinable physical or mental characteristic Exclusions: domestic employment

Table D.1 (continued)

State	Legislation	Current covered employer, definitions of disability, and exceptions
Minnesota	Human Rights Chapter 363 Division 03 Department of Human Rights Disability language added in 1973 Source: Minnesota Statutes Annotated, Volume 22B (1991).	Employer: a person who has one or more employees Disability: a physical, sensory or mental impairment which materially limits one or more major life activities, has record of or is regarded as having such an impairment Exclusions: family employment, domestic employment, religious and certain other associations
Mississippi	Title 43 Public Welfare, Chapter 6 Rights and Liabilities of Blind and Other Handicapped Persons, Article 1 General Provisions, Section 15 Employment Discrimination Act passed in 1974 (public employers only) Source: West's Mississippi Code Annotated, Volume 14 (1999).	Employers: state service, political subdivisions, public schools, employment supported whole or in part by public funds No other definitions available

Table D.1 (continued)

State	Legislation	Current covered employer, definitions of disability, and exceptions
Missouri	Title 12 Public Health and Welfare, Chapter 213, Human Rights Language to include handicap added in 1978. Source: Vernon's Annotated Missouri Statutes, Volume 12B 1999 Cumulative Annual Pocket Part. Title 12 Public Health and Welfare, Chapter 209 Aid to the Blind—Rights of Persons With Visual, Hearing or Physical Disabilities, Section 180 Section added in 1977 (public employers only) Source: Vernon's Annotated Missouri Statutes, Volume 12A 1996.	Employer: includes state, political division, any person employing six or more persons within the state and any person acting directly in the interest of an employer Disability: physical or mental impairment which substantially limits one or more of a person's major life activities, being regarded as having such an impairment or a record of such impairment which with or without reasonable accommodation does not interfere with performing the job Exclusions: religious or sectarian corporations and associations
Montana	Title 49 Human Rights Enacted in 1974 with handicap provisions in place Source: Montana Code Annotated 1991, Volume 8.	Employer: an employer of one or more persons or an agent of the employer Disability: physical or mental impairment, a record of or a condition regarded as such an impairment Exclusions: associations for nonprofit or those providing exclusive membership services

Table D.1 (continued)

State	Legislation	Current covered employer, definitions of disability, and exceptions
Nebraska	Chapter 48, Labor, Article 11 Nebraska Fair Employment Practice Act Disability provisions added in 1973. Source: Revised Statutes of Nebraska Annotated, Volume 12 (1995). Chapter 20 Civil Rights, Article 1 Individual Rights, (B) Persons with Disabilities, Section 131 Employment by State and Political Subdivisions; Policy Act passed in 1971 (public employers only) Source: Revised Statutes of Nebraska Annotated, Volume 14A (1999) Replacement Volume.	Employer: a person engaged in an industry who has 15 or more employees, 20 or more calendar weeks, any agent of such a person, any party whose business is financed in part or whole under the Nebraska Investment Finance Act regardless of number of employees; includes state, agencies and political subdivisions Disability: physical or mental impairment that substantially limits one or more of the major life activities of such an individual, a record of such or being regarded as having such an impairment Exclusions: U.S.A., U.S. government corporations, Indian tribe corporations, bona fide private membership clubs exempt from taxation, religious organizations, family employment, domestic employment
Nevada	Title 53 Labor and Industrial Relations, Chapter 613-Employment Practices, Equal Opportunities for Employment Handicapped language and provisions added in 1971 Source: Nevada Revised Statutes Annotated, Volume 16 (1996).	Employer: any person who has 15 or more employees for 20 weeks in current or previous year Disability: physical or mental impairment that substantially limits one or more of the major life activities of the person, a record of such an impairment or being regarded as having such an impairment Exclusions: U.S.A., U.S. government corporations, Indian tribes, tax exempt private membership clubs, religious organizations

Table D.1 (continued)

State	Legislation	Current covered employer, definitions of disability, and exceptions
New Hampshire	Title 31, Trade and Commerce, Chapter 354A State Commission for Human Rights, Equal Employment Opportunity	Employer: employs six or more persons, all state, political subdivisions, boards, departments and commissions thereof
	Law against discrimination regarding physical or mental handicap approved June 23, 1975	Disability: physical or mental impairment which substantially limits one or more of such person's major life activities, a record of having such an impairment or being regarded as having such an impairment
	Source: New Hampshire Revised Statutes Annotated 1995, Title 31.	
		Exclusions: social clubs, fraternal, charitable, educational or religious associations, and nonprofit corporations
New Jersey	Title 10 Civil Rights, Chapter 5 Law against Discrimination, Section 29.1	Employer: all corporations and organizations including the state, any political or civil subdivision thereof, and all public officers, agencies, boards, or bodies
	Last amendments effective March 2, 1978	
	Source: New Jersey Statutes Annotated, Title 9–11A (1993).	Disability: suffering from physical disability, infirmity, malformation or disfigurement etc., includes HIV/AIDS sufferers
		Exclusions: domestic servant and family employment

Table D.1 (continued)

State	Legislation	Current covered employer, definitions of disability, and exceptions
New Mexico	Chapter 28 Human Rights, Article 1 Human Rights Handicap language added in 1973. Act effective until July 1, 2000 Source: New Mexico Statutes 1978 Annotated, Volume 5, 1996 Replacement Pamphlet.	Employer: any person employing four or more persons and any person acting for an employer Disability: physical or mental impairment that substantially limits one or more of an individual's major life activities, has record of or is regarded as having such Exclusions: no exclusions available
New York	Article 15 Human Rights Law Disability language added in 1974 Source: McKinney's Consolidated Laws of New York Annotated, Book 18, Executive Law (1993).	Employer: minimum four employees Disability: physical, mental or medical impairment, a record of such impairment, or a condition regarded by others as such an impairment Exclusions: family or domestic employment
North Carolina	Chapter 168A Handicapped Persons Protection Act Act passed in 1985 with provisions in place Source: General Statutes of North Carolina Annotated, Volume 21, Chapters 160–168A (1944–1999).	Employer: any person employing 15 or more full-time employees within the state Disability: any person who has a physical or mental impairment which substantially limits one or more major life activities, has a record of such impairment, or is regarded as having such an impairment Exclusions: domestic or farm workers at that person's home or farm

Table D.1 (continued)

State	Legislation	Current covered employer, definitions of disability, and exceptions
North Dakota	Title 14 Domestic Relations and Persons, Chapter 14–02.4 Human Rights Initially passed in 1983 Source: North Dakota Century Code Annotated, Volume 3A, 1997 Replacement.	Employer: person within the state who employs one or more employees for more than one quarter of the year within the state and a person wherever situated who employs one or more employees whose services are to be partially or wholly performed in the state Disability: physical or mental impairment that substantially limits one or more major life activities, a record of impairment, or being regarded as having impairment Exclusions: elected public officials, person chosen by the officer/an appointee, or advisor (as employees)
Ohio	Title 41 Labor and Industry, Chapter 4112 Civil Rights Commission Language in place in 1976 Source: Page's Ohio Revised Code Annotated, Title 41 Labor and Industry, 1998 Replacement Volume.	Employer: includes state, any political subdivision of the state, any person employing four or more persons within the state, and any person acting directly or indirectly in the interest of an employer Disability: physical or mental impairment that substantially limits one or more major life activities, has record or is regarded as having such an impairment Exclusions: domestic service

Table D.1 (continued)

State	Legislation	Current covered employer, definitions of disability, and exceptions
Oklahoma	Title 25 Definitions and General Provisions, Chapter 21 Discrimination, Article 3 Discrimination in Employment In 1981 language added definition and prohibited handicap discrimination Source: Oklahoma Statutes Annotated (1987).	Employer: person who has 15 or more employees, 20 or more calendar weeks, includes contractor/subcontractor for the state or a government entity or agency of the state and includes agent of such a person Disability: physical or mental impairment which substantially limits one or more of such person's major life activities, has a record of or is regarded as having such an impairment Exclusions: Indian tribes, nonprofit bona fide membership club, family, domestic and religious employment
Oregon	Title 51 (Part 2) Labor and Industrial Relations, Chapter 659 Enforcement of Civil Rights; Unlawful Employment Practices, Civil Rights of Physically and Mentally Handicapped Language added in 1973 Source: Oregon Revised Statutes Annotated (1989).	Employer: any person that employs six or more persons and includes the state, counties, cities, districts, authorities, public corporations and entities and their instrumentalities Disability: physical or mental impairment which substantially limits one or more major life activities, has record or is regarded as having such an impairment Exclusions: Oregon National Guard

Table D.1 (continued)

State	Legislation	Current covered employer, definitions of disability, and exceptions
Pennsylvania	Title 43 Labor, Chapter 17 Human Relations 1974 amendment included disability Source: Purdon's Pennsylvania Statutes Annotated, Title 43–45 (1991).	Employer: includes commonwealth and any political subdivision, board, department, commission, school district thereof and any person employing four or more persons, includes religious, fraternal, charitable and sectarian corporations and associations Disability: No definition of disability Exclusions: corporations or associations supported in whole or part by governmental appropriations
Rhode Island	Title 28 Labor and Labor Relations, Chapter 5 Fair Employment Practices In 1973 initially added language of physical handicap Source: General Laws of Rhode Island 1956, Reenactment Code of 1995, Volume 5.	Employer: includes the state and all political subdivisions thereof and any person in the state employing four or more individuals and any person acting in the interest of an employer directly or indirectly Disability: physical or mental impairment which substantially limits one or more major life activities, has a record of or is regarded as having an impairment Exclusions: family and domestic employment, religious organization

Table D.1 (continued)

State	Legislation	Current covered employer, definitions of disability, and exceptions
South Carolina	Title 1 Administration of the Government, Chapter 13 State Human Affairs Commission	Employer: any person who has 15 or more employees, 20 or more calendar weeks, any agent of such a person
	July 6, 1996, amendments included prohibition of discrimination based on disability, declaring it an unlawful employment practice	Disability: physical or mental impairment that substantially limits one or more major life activities, has a record of or is regarded as having an impairment
	Source: Code of Laws of South Carolina 1976, Volume 1, 1998 Cumulative Supplement.	Exclusions: Indian tribes and bona fide private membership clubs, elected public officials, or any person chosen by such officer
	Title 43 Social Services, Chapter 33 Rights of Physically Disabled Persons, Article 1 In General, Section 60 Policy regarding employment of blind and other physically disabled persons	
	Article in place in 1972 (public employers only)	
	Source: Code of Laws of South Carolina 1976, Volume 15.	

Table D.1 (continued)

State	Legislation	Current covered employer, definitions of disability, and exceptions
South Dakota	Title 20 Personal Rights and Obligations, Chapter 13 Human Rights Previous act regarded employment discrimination based on blindness or partial blindness in 1984. General term "disability" added in 1986 Source: South Dakota Codified Laws, Volume 7A, 1995 Revision. Title 3 Public Officers and Employees, Chapter 3–6A Career Service Personnel Management System, Section 15 Discrimination Prohibited—Violation Misdemeanor Act established in 1973 (public employers only) Source: South Dakota Codified Laws, Volume 2B, 1994 Revision.	Employee: any person who performs services for any employer for compensation, no minimum number of employees Disability: physical or mental impairment which substantially limits one or more of the person's major life functions, having record of such or being regarded as having such an impairment Exclusions: qualifications based on religious purpose
Tennessee	Title 8 Public Officers and Employees, Chapter 50 Miscellaneous Provisions, Part 1 General Provisions Legislation initially passed in 1976 Source: Tennessee Code Annotated Volume 3, 1993 Replacement.	No definitions available

Table D.1 (continued)

State	Legislation	Current covered employer, definitions of disability, and exceptions
Texas	Title 2 Protection of Laborers, Subtitle A Employment Discrimination, Chapter 21 Employment Discrimination, Subchapter B Unlawful Employment Practices Language added in 1989 Source: Vernon's Texas Code Annotated, Labor Code, Volume 1 (1996).	Employer: a person who is engaged in industry affecting commerce and who has 15 or more employees, 20 or more calendar weeks; an agent of, or an elected public official; includes a county, municipality, state agency, or state instrumentality, including public institution of education, regardless of the number of employees Disability: physical or mental impairment which substantially limits at least one major life activity of an individual, a record of such impairment, or being regarded as having such Exclusions: elected public officials (as employees)
Utah	Title 34A Utah Labor Code, Chapter 5 Utah Antidiscrimination Act Language added in 1979 Source: Utah Code Annotated 1953, Volume 4B, 1997 Replacement.	Employer: the state or any political subdivision or board, commission, department institution, school district, trust, or agent thereof, and every other person employing 15 or more employees, 20 calendar weeks Disability: physical or mental impairment which substantially limits one or more of a person's major life activities Exclusions: religious entities

Table D.1 (continued)

State	Legislation	Current covered employer, definitions of disability, and exceptions
Vermont	Title 21 Labor, Chapter 5 Employment Practices, Subchapter 6 Fair Employment Practices Language added in 1981 Source: Vermont Statutes Annotated 1987.	Employer: any individual, organization, or governmental body including partnership, association, trustee, estate, corporation, joint stock company, insurance company, or legal representative, whether domestic or foreign, or the receiver, trustee in bankruptcy, trustee or successor thereof, and any common carrier by mail, motor, water, air or express company doing business in or operating within the state which has one or more individuals Disability: any person who has a physical or mental impairment which substantially limits one or more major life activities, has a history or record of such or is regarded as having such Exclusions: no exclusions available
Virginia	Title 51.5 Persons with Disabilities Previous title passed in 1972 (public employers only) Source: Code of Virginia 1950 Annotated, Volume 7A, 1998 Replacement Volume.	Employer: the state or entity funded Disability: any person who has physical or mental impairment which substantially limits one or more major life activities, or having record of such Exclusions: employers covered by the Federal Rehabilitation Act of 1973

Table D.1 (continued)

State	Legislation	Current covered employer, definitions of disability, and exceptions
Washington	Title 49 Labor Regulations, Chapter 60 Discrimination—Human Rights Commission Added disability section in 1973 Source: West's Revised Code of Washington Annotated Titles 49–50 (1990).	Employer: any person acting in the interest of the employer, directly or indirectly, who employs eight or more persons Disability: no definition of disability Exclusions: nonprofit religious or sectarian organizations, family and domestic employment
Washington, D.C.	Title 1 Administration, Chapter 25 Human Rights Subchapter II Prohibited Acts of Discrimination Effective 1994 Source: DC Code Annotated, 1981 Edition, Volume 2A, 1999 Replacement. Title 16 Health and Safety, Chapter 17 Rights of the Blind and Physically Disabled Persons, Section 5 Discrimination in Employment Prohibited Likely in place in 1972 (unable to verify) (pubic employers and employers receiving appropriations for D.C. only) Source: DC Code Annotated, 1981 Edition, Volume 4, 1995 Replacement .	Employer: any person who, for compensation employs an individual, any agent of such an employer and any professional association Disability: a physical or mental impairment that substantially limits one or more of the major life activities of an individual having a record of such an impairment or being regarded as having such an impairment Exclusions: family and domestic employment

Table D.1 (continued)

State	Legislation	Current covered employer, definitions of disability, and exceptions
West Virginia	Chapter 5 General Powers and Authority of the Governor, Secretary of State and Attorney General, Board of Public Works; Miscellaneous Agencies, Commissions, Offices, Programs, Etc., Article 11 Human Rights Commission Handicap provisions added in 1981 Source: Michie's West Virginia Code Annotated, Volume 2, 1999 Replacement Volume.	Employer: the state, any political subdivision thereof, and person employing 12 or more employees, 20 calendar weeks Disability: physical or mental impairment which substantially limits one or more of such person's major life activities, a record of such impairment, or being regarded as having such Exclusions: private clubs and family employment
Wisconsin	Chapter 111 Employment Relations, Subchapter II Fair Employment Section amended to include the word handicap in 1965 Source: West's Wisconsin Statutes Annotated (1997).	Employer: the state and each agency of the state, and any other person engaging in any activity, enterprise or business employing at least one individual Disability: physical or mental impairment which makes achievement unusually difficult or limits the capacity to work, has a record of such impairment, or is perceived as having such Exclusions: social club or fraternal society, family employment

Table D.1 (continued)

State	Legislation	Current covered employer, definitions of disability, and exceptions
Wyoming	Title 27 Labor and Employment, Chapter 9 Fair Employment Practices Language added in 1985 Source: Wyoming Statutes Annotated, 1999 Edition Volume 6.	Employer: the state or any political subdivision or board, commission, department, institution, or school district thereof, and every other person employing two or more employees Disability: no definition of disability Exclusions: religious organizations or associations

NOTE: It is typical for legislation to allow for discrimination based on ability to perform the job and to define a *qualified* disabled person as one who can perform the job with reasonable accommodation.

References

Acemoglu, Daron, and Joshua Angrist. 2001. "Consequences of Employment Protection? The Case of the Americans with Disabilities Act." *Journal of Political Economy* 109(5): 915–957.

Advisory Commission on Intergovernmental Relations. 1989. *Disability Rights Mandates: Federal and State Compliance with Employment Protections and Architectural Barrier Removal*, report A-111. Washington, D.C.: Advisory Commission on Intergovernmental Relations.

Akerlof, George A., and Brian G.M. Main. 1981. "An Experience-Weighted Measure of Employment and Unemployment Duration." *American Economic Review* 71(5): 1003–1011.

Altonji, Joseph G., and Christina H. Paxson. 1988. "Labor Supply Preferences, Hours Constraints, and Hours-Wage Tradeoffs." *Journal of Labor Economics* 6(2): 254–276.

Americans with Disabilities Act of 1990 (July 26 1990). 42 US Code 12101, Sec. (2). Also see <http://www.eeoc.gov/laws/ada.html>.

Autor, David H., and Mark Duggan. 2001. "The Rise in Disability Recipiency and the Decline in Unemployment." Working paper no. 01-15, Massachusetts Institute of Technology, Cambridge, Massachusetts.

Averett, Susan L., and Julie L. Hotchkiss. 1995. "The Probability of Receiving Benefits at Different Hours of Work." *American Economic Review* 85(2): 276–280.

———. 1996. "Discrimination through Payment of Full-time Wage Premiums." *Industrial and Labor Relations Review* 49(2): 287–301.

———. 1997. "Female Labor Supply with a Discontinuous, Non-Convex Budget Constraint: Incorporation of a Full-Time/Part-Time Wage Differential." *Review of Economics and Statistics* 79(3): 461–470.

Averett, Susan L., Richard Warner, Jani Little, and Peter Huxley. 1999. "Labor Supply, Disabiity Benefits, and Mental Illness." *Eastern Economic Journal* 25(3): 279–288.

Baldwin, Marjorie L. 1999. "The Effects of Impairments on Employment and Wages: Estimates from the 1984 and 1990 SIPP." *Behavioral Sciences and the Law* 17(1): 7–27.

Baldwin, Marjorie L., and William G. Johnson. 1995. "Labor Market Discrimination against Women with Disabilities." *Industrial Relations* 34(4): 555–577.

———. 2000. "Labor Market Discrimination against Men with Disabilities in the Year of the ADA." *Southern Economic Journal* 66(3): 548–566.

Baldwin, Marjorie L. and Edward J. Schumacher. 1999. "Job Mobility among Workers with Disabilities." Working Paper, East Carolina University, Greenville, South Carolina.

Ben-Akiva, Moshe, and Steven R. Lerman. 1985. *Discrete Choice Analysis: Theory and Application to Travel Demand.* Cambridge, Massachusetts: MIT Press.

Blank, Rebecca M. 1990. "Are Part-time Jobs Bad Jobs?" In *A Future of Lousy Jobs? The Changing Structure of U.S. Wages,* Gary Burtless, ed. Washington, D.C.: Brookings Institute, pp. 123–155.

Bortnick, Steven M., and Michelle Harrison Ports. 1992. "Job Search Methods and Results: Tracking the Unemployed, 1991." *Monthly Labor Review* 115(12): 29–35.

Bound, John, and Timothy Waidmann. 2002. "Accounting for Recent Declines in Employment Rates among the Working-Aged Men and Women with Disabilities." *Journal of Human Resources* 37(2): 231–250.

Buchmueller, Thomas C., and Robert G. Valletta. 1996. "The Effects of Employer-Provided Health Insurance on Worker Mobility." *Industrial and Labor Relations Review* 49(3): 439–455.

Burkhauser, Richard V., J. S. Butler, and Yang Woo Kim. 1995. "The Importance of Employer Accommodation on the Job Duration of Workers with Disabilities: A Hazard Model Approach." *Labour Economics* 2(2): 109–130.

Burkhauser, Richard V., Mary C. Daly, and Andrew J. Houtenville. 2000. "How Working Age People with Disabilities Fared over the 1990s Business Cycle." Working paper, Rehabilitation Research and Training Center for Economic Research on Employment Policy for Persons with Disabilities, Cornell University, Ithaca, New York.

———. 2001. "The Emploment of Working-Age People with Disabilities in the 1980s and 1990s: What Current Data Cannot Tell Us." Working paper, Federal Reserve Bank of San Francisco, San Francisco, California.

Burkhauser, Richard V., Andrew Glenn, and David C. Wittenburg. 1997. "The Disabled Worker Tax Credit." In *Disability: Challenges for Social Insurance, Health Care Financing, and Labor Market Policy,* Virginia Reno, Jerry Mashaw, and William Gradison, eds. Washington, D.C.: National Academy of Social Insurance, pp. 47–65.

Burkhauser, Richard V., Robert H. Haveman, and Barbara L. Wolfe. 1993. "How People with Disabilities Fare When Public Policies Change." *Journal of Policy Analysis and Management* 12(2): 251–269.

Card, David. 1992. "The Effects of Minimum Wage Legislation: A Case Study of California, 1987–89." *Industrial and Labor Relations Review* 46(1): 38–54.

Carrington, William J., Kristin McCue, and Brooks Pierce. 2000. "Using Establishment Size to Measure the Impact of Title VII and Affirmative Action." *Journal of Human Resources* 35(3): 503–523.

Chatterjee, Lata, and Monika Mitra. 1998. "Evolution of Federal and State Policies for Persons with Disability in the United States: Efficiency and Welfare Impacts." *Annals of Regional Science* 32(3): 347–365.

Chay, Kenneth Young. 1996. "An Empirical Analysis of Black Economic Progress over Time." Ph.D. dissertation, Princeton University, Princeton, New Jersey.

Chen, Edwin. 2001. "Bush Initiative Targets Barriers to the Disabled." *Los Angeles Times*, February 2: A21.

Chirikos, Thomas N. 1991. "The Economics of Employment." In *The Americans with Disabilities Act: From Policy to Practice*, Jane West, ed. New York: Milbank Memorial Fund, pp. 150–179.

Condrey, Stephen E., and Jeffrey L. Brudney. 1998. "The Americans with Disabilities Act of 1990: Assessing Its Implementation in America's Largest Cities." *American Review of Public Administration* 28(1): 26–42.

Cotton, Jeremiah. 1988. "On the Decomposition of Wage Differentials." *Review of Economics and Statistics* 70(2): 236–243.

Davies, Paul, Howard Iams, and Kalman Rupp. 2000. "The Effect of Welfare Reform on SSA's Disability Programs: Design of Policy Evaluation and Early Evidence." *Social Security Bulletin* 63(1): 3–11.

DeLeire, Thomas. 2001. "Changes in Wage Discrimination against People with Disabilities: 1984–93." *Journal of Human Resources* 36(1): 144–158.

DeLeire, Thomas Charles. 1997. "The Wages and Employment Effects of the Americans with Disabilities Act." Ph.D. dissertation, Stanford University, Palo Alto, California.

———. 2000. "The Wages and Employment Effects of the Americans with Disabilities Act." *Journal of Human Resources* 35(4): 693–715.

Donohue, John J., and James Heckman. 1991. "Continuous versus Episodic Change: The Impact of Civil Rights Policy on the Economic Status of Blacks." *Journal of Economic Literature* 29(4): 1603–1643.

DuMouchel, William H., and Greg J. Duncan. 1983. "Using Sample Survey Weights in Multiple Regression Analysis of Stratified Samples." *Journal of the American Statistical Association* 78(383): 535–543.

Duncan, Otis Dudley, and Beverly Duncan. 1955. "A Methodological Analysis of Segregation Indexes." *American Sociological Review* 20(2): 210–217.

Dykxhoorn, Hans J., and Kathleen E. Sinning. 1993. "Complying with the Americans with Disabilities Act: Costs and Tax Treatment." *The National Public Accountant* 38(6): 32–34.

Ellner, Jack R., and Henry E. Bender. 1980. *Hiring the Handicapped.* New York: AMACOM.

Farber, Henry S., and Helen Levy. 2000. "Recent Trends in Employer-Sponsored Health Insurance Coverage: Are Bad Jobs Getting Worse?" *Journal of Health Economics* 19(1): 93–119.

Ginther, Donna K., and Kathy J. Hayes. 2001. "Gender Differences in Salary and Promotion for Faculty in the Humanities, 1977–95." Working paper no. 2001-7, Federal Reserve Bank of Atlanta, Atlanta, Georgia.

Green, David A. 1999. "Immigrant Occupational Attainment: Assimilation and Mobility over Time." *Journal of Labor Economics* 17(1): 49–79.

Gruber, Jonathan. 1994. "The Incidence of Mandated Maternity Benefits." *American Economic Review* 84(3): 622–641.

———. 1996. "Disability Insurance Benefits and Labor Supply." Working paper no. 5866, National Bureau of Economic Research, Cambridge, Massachusetts.

Gunderson, Morley, and Douglas Hyatt. 1996. "Do Injured Workers Pay for Reasonable Accommodation?" *Industrial and Labor Relations Review* 50(1): 92–104.

Hale, Thomas W. 2001. "The Lack of a Disability Measure in Today's Current Population Survey." *Monthly Labor Review* 124(6): 38–40.

Hamermesh, Daniel S., and Stephen J. Trejo. 2000. "The Demand for Hours of Labor: Direct Evidence from California." *Review of Economics and Statistics* 82(1): 38–47.

Haveman, Robert, and Barbara Wolfe. 1984. "The Decline in Male Labor Force Participation: Comment." *Journal of Political Economy* 92(3): 532–541.

———. 1990. "The Economic Well-Being of the Disabled: 1962–84." *Journal of Human Resources* 25(1): 32–54.

Hays, Scott. 1999. "Tax Incentives Can Offset the Cost of ADA Compliance." *Workforce* 78(7): 84.

Heckman, James. 1979. "Sample Selection Bias as a Specification Error." *Econometrica* 47(1): 153–161.

———. 1996. "Comment." In *Tax Policy and The Economy*, James M. Poterba, ed. Cambridge, Massachusetts: MIT Press, pp. 32–38.

Hollenbeck, Kevin, and Jean Kimmel. 2001. "The Returns to Education and Basic Skills Training for Individuals with Poor Health or Disability." Working paper no. WP01-72, W.E. Upjohn Institute for Employment Research, Kalamazoo, Michigan.

Horvath, Francis, and Marquez Janice Shack. 1986. *Accepted Wages: Examining Transitions from Unemployment and out of the Labor Force.* Working paper no. 62, Board of Governors of the Federal Reserve System, Economic Activity Section, Washington, D.C.

Hotchkiss, Julie L. 1991. "The Definition of Part-Time Employment: A Switching Regression Model with Unknown Sample Selection." *International Economic Review* 32(4): 899–917.

Jay, Leslie. 1990. "The Americans with Disabilities Act: Feel-Good Legislation?" *Management Review* 79(9): 22–24.

Johnson, Mark. 1997. "Companies' Big Mistake Might Be Avoiding ADA." *The Tampa Tribune*, August 24.

Johnson, William G., and James Lambrinos. 1985. "Wage Discrimination against Handicapped Men and Women." *Journal of Human Resources* 20(2): 264–277.

Kalbfleisch, John D., and Ross L. Prentice. 1980. *The Statistical Analysis of Failure Time Data.* New York: Wiley and Sons.

Kapur, Kanika. 1998. "The Impact of Health on Job Mobility: A Measure of Job Lock." *Industrial and Labor Relations Review* 51(2): 282–298.

Katz, Lawrence. 1998. "Wage Subsidies for the Disadvantaged." In *Generating Jobs: How to Increase Demand for Less Skilled Workers*, Richard B. Freeman and Peter Gottschalk, eds. New York: Russell Sage, pp. 21–53.

Kaufman, Bruce E., and Julie L. Hotchkiss. 2000. *The Economics of Labor Markets*, Fifth ed. Fort Worth, Texas: Dryden Press.

Kaye, Steven. 2002. "Improved Employment Opportunities for People with Disabilities." Working paper, Disability Statistics Center, University of California-San Francisco, San Francisco, California.

Kiefer, Nicholas M. 1988. "Economic Duration Data and Hazard Functions." *Journal of Economic Literature* 26(2): 646–679.

Kiefer, Nicholas, Shelly J. Lundberg, and George R. Neumann. 1985. "How Long Is a Spell of Unemployment? Illusions and Biases in the Use of CPS Data." *Journal of Business and Economic Statistics* 3(2): 118–128.

Kirchner, Corinne. 1996. "Looking under the Street Lamp: Inappropriate Uses of Measures Just Because They Are There." *Journal of Disability Policy Studies* 7(1): 77–90.

Kreider, Brent. 1999. "Latent Work Disability and Reporting Bias." *Journal of Human Resources* 34(4): 734–769.

Kruse, Douglas, and Lisa Schur. 2002. *Employment of People with Disabilities following the ADA.* Working paper, Rutgers University School of Management and Labor Relations, New Brunswick, New Jersey.

Kubik, Jeffrey D. 1999. "Incentives for the Identification and Treatment of Children with Disabilities: The Supplemental Security Income Program." *Journal of Public Economics* 73 (2): 187–215.

Kujala, Oliver A. 1996. "The Bottom Line on ADA." *CFO* 12(5): 12.

Landes, William M., and Lewis C. Solmon. 1972. "Compulsory Schooling Legislation: An Economic Analysis of Law and Social Change in the Nineteenth Century." *Journal of Economic History* 22(1): 54–91.

LaPlante, Alice. 1992. "Attitudes Still a Barrier for the Disabled." *Computerworld* 26(30): 30.

Lewin Group. 1999. *Policy Evaluation of the Overall Effects of Welfare Reform on SSA Programs: Final Report* (prepared for the Social Security Administration, April 23).

Long, J. Scott. 1997. *Regression Models for Categorical and Limited Dependent Variables.* Thousand Oaks, California: Sage Publications.

Lundberg, Shelly. 1985. "Tied Wage-Hours Offers and the Endogeneity of Wages." *Review of Economics and Statistics* 67 (3): 405–410.

Magill, Barbara Gambie. 1997. "ADA Accommodations Don't Have to Break the Bank." *HRMagazine* 42(7): 85–88.

Manski, Charles F., and David McFadden. 1981. *Structural Analysis of Discrete Data with Econometric Applications.* Cambridge, Massachusetts: MIT Press.

McNeil, John M. 2000. "Employment, Earnings, and Disability." Paper presented at the Western Economic Association Meeting, Vancouver, B.C.

Moehling, Carolyn M. 1999. "State Child Labor Laws and the Decline of Child Labor." *Explorations in Economic History* 36(1): 72–106.

Moffitt, Robert A. 1984. "The Estimation of a Joint Wage-Hours Labor Supply Model." *Journal of Labor Economics* 2(47): 550–566.

———. 1999. "New Developments in Econometric Methods for Labor Market Analysis." In *Handbook of Labor Economics.* Vol. 3, Orley Ashenfelter and David Card, eds. Amsterdam: North-Holland, pp. 1367–1397.

Murphy, Kevin M., Chinhui Juhn, and Brooks Pierce. 1993. "Wage Inequality and the Rise in Returns to Skill." *Journal of Political Economy* 101(3): 410–442.

Oaxaca, Ronald L., and Michael R. Ransom. 1994. "On Discrimination and the Decomposition of Wage Differentials." *Journal of Econometrics* 61 (1): 5–21.

O'Hara, Brian James. 2000. "Discrimination Against Persons with Disabilities: Issues in Employment Transistions." Ph.D. dissertation, University of Notre Dame, Indiana.

Parsons, Donald. 1980. "The Decline in Male Labor Force Participation." *Journal of Political Economy* 88(1): 117–134.

Polivka, Anne E. 1996. "Data Watch: The Redesigned Current Population Survey." *Journal of Economic Perspectives* 10(3): 169–180.

Roper Center for Public Opinion Research. 1999. Harris Poll, May 12. University of Connecticut, Storrs.

Rosen, Sherwin. 1991. "Disability Accommodation and the Labor Market" In *Disability and Work: Incentives, Rights, and Opportunities*, Carolyn L. Weaver, ed. Washington, D.C.: AEI Press, pp. 18–30.

Salkever, David S., and Marisa E. Domino. 1997. "Within Group 'Structural' Tests of Labor-Market Discrimination: A Study of Persons with Serious Disabilities." Working paper no. 5931, National Bureau of Economic Research, Cambridge, Massachusetts.

Scheid, Teresa L. 1998. "The Americans with Disabilities Act, Mental Disability and Employment Practices." *Journal of Behavioral Health Services and Research* 25(3): 312–324.

Schur, Lisa A. 2002. "Contingent and Part-Time Work among People with Disabilities: Barriers or Opportunities?" Working paper, Rutgers University.

Schwochau, Susan, and David Blanck. 2000. "The Economics of the Americans with Disabilities Act, Part III: Does the ADA Disable the Disabled?" *Berkeley Journal of Employment and Labor Law* 21(1): 271–314.

Sider, Hal. 1985. "Unemployment Duration and Incidence: 1968–82." *American Economic Review* 75(3): 41–72.

Social Security Administration. 2000. *Social Security Administration's Report on Supplemental Security Income: Income and Resource Exclusions and Disability Insurance Earning-Related Provisions.* Washington, D.C.: Social Security Adminstration.

Stern, Steven. 1989. "Measuring the Effect of Disability on Labor Force Participation." *Journal of Human Resources* 24 (3): 361–395.

———. 1996. "Semiparametric Estimates of the Supply and Demand Effects of Disability on Labor Force Participation." *Journal of Econometrics* 71 (1–2): 49–70.

Stratton, Leslie S. 1994. "Reexamining Involuntary and Part-time Employment." *Journal of Economic and Social Measurement* 20(2): 95–113.

Tannenwald, Robert. 1982. "Are Wage and Training Subsidies Cost Effective? Some Evidence from the New Jobs Tax Credit." *New England Economic Review* (September/October): 25–34.

Thomas, Jonathan. 1991. "Main Search Methods and Outcomes." Working paper no. 9119, University of Cambridge Department of Applied Economics, Cambridge, England.

Tummers, Martijn P., and Isolde Woittiez. 1991. "A Simultaneous Wage and Labor Supply Model with Hours Restrictions." *Journal of Human Resources* 26(3): 394–423.

Veum, Jonathan R., and Andrea B. Weiss. 1993. "Education and the Work Histories of Young Adults." *Monthly Labor Review* 116(4): 11–20.

U.S. Department of Labor, Bureau of Labor Statistics. 2001. *Employment and Earnings.* Washington, D.C.: Bureau of Labor Statistics.

Watts, Martin. 1992. "How Should Occupational Sex Segregation Be Measured?" *Work, Employment and Society* 6(3): 475–487.

Wooldridge, Jeffrey M. 1999. "Asymptotic Properties of Weighted M-Estimators for Variable Probability Samples." *Econometrica* 67(6): 1385–1406.

Yelin, Edward H. 1991. "The Recent History and Immediate Future of Employment among Persons with Disabilities." In *The Americans with Disabilities Act: From Policy to Practice*, Jane West, ed. New York: Milbank Memorial Fund, pp. 129–149.

Yelin, Edward, and Mirium Cisternas. 1996. "The Contemporary Labor Market and the Employment Prospects of Persons with Disabilities." In *Disability, Work, and Cash Benefits*, Jerry L. Mashaw, Virginia Reno, Richard V. Burkhauser, and Monroe Berkowitz, eds. Kalamazoo, Michigan: W.E. Upjohn Institute for Employment Research, pp. 33–58.

Zveglich, Joseph E., Jr., and Yana van der Meulen Rodgers. 1996. "The Impact of Protective Measures for Female Workers: Some Evidence from Taiwan." Working paper, Department of Economics, College of William and Mary, Williamsburg, Virgina.

The Author

Julie L. Hotchkiss is an Associate Professor of Economics in the Andrew Young School of Policy Studies at Georgia State University. She received her B.A. degree from Willamette University in 1985, and her Ph.D. in Economics from Cornell University in 1989. Hotchkiss has published numerous articles on a variety of topics, including the relationship among state unemployment rates, wage differentials in Jamaica, labor supply behavior and welfare of two-earner families, the impact of unemployment insurance programs on individual job search behavior, and wage determination of part-time workers. She is also co-author of one of the leading Labor Economics textbooks. It is with great enthusiasm that she brings her varied skills and experience to the important subject of workers with disabilities. In addition to her professional activities, she counts among her greatest accomplishments her marriage of 15 years and her two terrific children.

Index

The italic letters *f*, *n*, and *t* following a page number indicate that the subject information is within a figure, note, or table, respectively, on that page.

About the Institute

The W.E. Upjohn Institute for Employment Research is a nonprofit research organization devoted to finding and promoting solutions to employment-related problems at the national, state, and local levels. It is an activity of the W.E. Upjohn Unemployment Trustee Corporation, which was established in 1932 to administer a fund set aside by the late Dr. W.E. Upjohn, founder of The Upjohn Company, to seek ways to counteract the loss of employment income during economic downturns.

The Institute is funded largely by income from the W.E. Upjohn Unemployment Trust, supplemented by outside grants, contracts, and sales of publications. Activities of the Institute comprise the following elements: 1) a research program conducted by a resident staff of professional social scientists; 2) a competitive grant program, which expands and complements the internal research program by providing financial support to researchers outside the Institute; 3) a publications program, which provides the major vehicle for disseminating the research of staff and grantees, as well as other selected works in the field; and 4) an Employment Management Services division, which manages most of the publicly funded employment and training programs in the local area.

The broad objectives of the Institute's research, grant, and publication programs are to 1) promote scholarship and experimentation on issues of public and private employment and unemployment policy, and 2) make knowledge and scholarship relevant and useful to policymakers in their pursuit of solutions to employment and unemployment problems.

Current areas of concentration for these programs include causes, consequences, and measures to alleviate unemployment; social insurance and income maintenance programs; compensation; workforce quality; work arrangements; family labor issues; labor-management relations; and regional economic development and local labor markets.